RUINED

RUINED

LYNN NOTTAGE

THEATRE COMMUNICATIONS GROUP
NEW YORK
2009

Ruined is published by Theatre Communications Group, Inc.,
520 Eighth Avenue, 24th Floor, New York, NY 10018-4156

This publication is made possible in part with public funds from the New
York State Council on the Arts, a State Agency.

TCG books are exclusively distributed to the book trade by Consortium Book
Sales and Distribution.

LIBRARY OF CONGRESS CATALOGING-IN-PUBLICATION DATA

Nottage, Lynn.
Ruined / Lynn Nottage. — 1st ed.
p. cm.
ISBN 978-1-55936-355-6 (pbk)
ISBN 978-1-55936-369-3 (cloth)
1. Brothels—Drama. 2. Congo (Democratic Republic)—Drama.   I. Title.
PS3564.O795R85 2009
812'.54—dc22
2009028210
CIP

Book design, composition and cover design by Lisa Govan
Cover and interior photos by Tony Gerber

First Edition, August 2009

For Ruby Gerber

My reason for optimism

CONTENTS

INTRODUCTION

By Kate Whoriskey

All of us who spend our lives in theater know that, at its core, this performing art is sacred. It has an incredible capacity for illuminating the unseen, reshaping history, bringing out empathy and providing social commentary. And yet it takes years in the trenches to develop a handful of meaningful productions. Once in a great while a project seems to get enough of the elements right that it becomes a memorable piece of theater. *Ruined* is one of those pieces.

How did it all begin?

Five years ago, Lynn and I were preparing for our second collaboration, *Fabulation*. On a break, we got into a conversation about Brecht and found that both of us admired *Mother Courage*. I have always been drawn to Brecht's heightened style and epic writing, and was compelled by the notion of staging a woman's complicated relationship to war. The cruel paradox of Mother Courage, a woman who profited from a war that took her children, seemed like fertile theatrical ground.

Lynn wanted to do a version of *Mother Courage* set in the Congo. A violent war over natural resources had been raging there for years, causing one of the highest death tolls of any war, and, yet, the violence generated very little media attention. Since her days working for Amnesty International, Lynn had been disturbed by the lack of interest the international community showed for such a devastating conflict. She thought that doing an adaptation might call attention to the crisis.

Months passed without further conversation about the transplanted *Mother Courage*. Then, one day, Lynn called me: "I bought a ticket to Uganda," she said, "do you want to go with me?" Lynn had chosen the bordering country of Uganda because the violence in the Congo had been heating up between the Hema and the Lendus and multiple other factions. There was an Amnesty International based in Kampala, Uganda, and she could use contacts to set up interviews with Congolese women who had crossed over the border to escape the violence. She had bought her ticket to leave the day after *Fabulation* rehearsals ended.

So we opened *Fabulation*, and the next day boarded a plane bound for Central Africa.

One of the first people we met in Kampala was a driver who said he was willing to take us anywhere, but also wanted to warn us about certain locations we chose. First on our itinerary was the refugee camp in Arva, north of Kampala. "I am willing to take you there. I do food runs there for various NGOs, but I want to let you know the violence is increasing there." He spoke of rebels cutting off women's tongues to upset the camps. The violence was reminiscent of explorer turned colonizer Henry Morton Stanley. A century ago, Stanley was responsible for securing free labor to support Belgian King Leopold II's rubber trade. To ensure cooperation, Stanley cut off the hands of anyone refusing to work. Such butchery, practiced by colonizers one hundred years earlier, seemed to influence current acts of violence in a post-colonial Congo.

The senseless yet targeted violence got me thinking about the women we were here to interview and what their stories were. I have often questioned why rape is an integral part of any war. After interviewing the women, I realized that it was not just a tool to humiliate the women or to degrade the opposing side's masculinity, it was a way to strip women of their wombs. All but one of the women interviewed were raped by multiple men. The physical damage incurred was so great that they were left without the ability to produce children.

Like many people who perpetrate sexual crimes, the men and boys who raped were themselves victims of unspeakable violence. Rebels interested in recruiting more soldiers would invade family houses and make boys kill their parents in order to save themselves. These boys became so damaged they would join the rebel group that forced them to make this unconscionable choice. When I spoke to Doctor Denis Mukwege, who is the lead doctor at Panzi hospital in Bukavu, in the Democratic Republic of Congo, I asked him if he ever met a boy who suffered this experience and was then rehabilitated. He answered no. Worse than a suicide bomber, these boys and men are so psychologically scarred that from the point of the trauma forward, they spend the rest of their lives terrorizing and destroying others.

Since our trip, I have been haunted by the human capacity to use creativity and imagination to such deadly ends. I would like to think that we are better off in the United States, but when you look at what was done in Abu Ghraib and Guantanamo Bay, we are only wealthy enough to keep it offshore. In the United States, we have the money to create weaponry that removes us from the violence we enact. By contrast, in the Congo, the mixture of poverty and war is a lethal combination. Due to a lack of money, the human body becomes the weapon, the teenage boy the terror, and a woman's womb "the battleground."

As we interviewed more and more people, it became clear that we did not want to be beholden to Brecht's ideas. Lynn was interested in portraying the lives of Central Africans as accurately as she could, and she found *Mother Courage* to be a false frame. She decided to abandon the idea of adaptation in favor of a structure that was true to our experiences in Uganda. What struck both of us from our trip was that while there was incredible chaos in the region, this was home, and people were determined to survive and build lives here. When the media focuses attention on these areas, they often describe the violence, the poverty and the AIDS crisis. It is rare to hear the full story, the positive alongside the negative.

What was so rich about our trip is that we witnessed great beauty, strength and artistry.

We met women who had formed a group called Isis, dedicated to documenting the violence against women and administering medical and psychological care to the communities that had been traumatized by armed conflicts. We met the phenomenal spirit of Doctor Mukwege, who dedicates his life to repairing the physical injuries of women. We met people who ran orphanages for children whose parents were lost to the war and AIDS. They took care of hundreds of orphans with respect and discipline. We also heard incredible music, saw stand-up comedians perform, bought and enjoyed hand-crafted masks, baskets, jewelry and textiles, drank Waragi, the local liquor, went on safari, took a white-water rafting trip down the Nile and hiked for hours to see the gorillas on the border of the Congo.

On a different trip to the region, Lynn spoke with a Rwandan about life after the genocide. He said to her, "We must fight to sustain the complexity." This phrase became a mantra for creating the piece. We did not want to focus solely on the damage but also the hope.

The core commitment of *Ruined* is to celebrate and examine the spectrum of human life in all its complexities: the sacred with the profane, the transcendent with the lethal, the flaws with the beauty, and selfishness with generosity.

Lynn has the gift and genius for looking inside moments of profound disruption, witnessing the chaos, absorbing the psychic damage, and then synthesizing a narrative that shows us we are capable of so much more.

Her writing not only provides the drama, it also gives all the clues so that one can tap into the contrasting elements. As a director committed to staging complexity, my task is to counter the drama with humor, spirit and wit, and to treat the stories collected in Central Africa with the understanding that at every moment the Congolese are determined to survive.

I am proud to have worked on a show that has gotten the attention of the United Nations and the United States Senate. Several delegates from the United Nations, including Secretary General Ban-Ki Moon, have attended the performance, as have human rights activists and organizations. Lynn Nottage and Quincy Tyler Bernstine were invited to attend the Senate Foreign Relations Committee hearing of the Subcommittee on International Operations and Organizations, Democracy, Human Rights and Global Women's Issues, and the Subcommittee on African Affairs, which was designed to examine the use of violence against women, particularly rape, as a tool of war in conflict zones and "to explore what steps are being taken to stop this horrific practice once and for all." Quincy Tyler Bernstine then presented Salima's Act Two monologue at a reception following that hearing.

These moments restore my faith that theater can activate change, heal a bit of the horror, restore hope and give voice to the silent and unseen.

It has been a privilege to work on this play with Lynn, the acting ensemble, the producers at Manhattan Theatre Club and the Goodman, and the design team. I am thankful that audiences are empathizing with the lives of people that news outlets typically avoid.

A friend of mine says that if you commit yourself to a life in theater, you may only make five to ten pieces that are truly momentous. I am glad to say that *Ruined* was one.

ACKNOWLEDGMENTS

A heartfelt thank you to the incredible Congolese women who bravely shared their stories. My play is a tribute to their tenacious spirits.

Some of the Congolese women who shared their narratives were: Shabaru Brigitte, Jeanne Kavira, Nya Kakoheryo, Sindje Tokoko Esther, Alimasi Mulemaza, Pauline Tamwe, Muzima Salima, Mama Nadi Zabibu, Abambu Josephine, Sophie Somana, Ntamusimwa Emilienne, Biswaza Mariah, Katungu Vihamba Rose and Bernadette Bwira Astride.

Special thanks:

To the phenomenal cast and crew of *Ruined*, Kate Whoriskey, Tony Gerber, Bob Falls, Roche Schulfer, Tanya Palmer, Dan Sullivan, Lynne Meadow, Barry Grove, Steve Scott, Mandy Greenfield, Jerry Patch, Lisa McNulty, Nancy Piccione, Peter Hagan, Jocelyn Clarke, LAByrinth Theater Company, Jessica Neuwirth, Taina Bien-Aime and Equality Now, Jane Saks and the Ellen Belic Stone Institute for the Study of Women and Gender in the Arts and Media, David Mukassa, Charles Dickens Elem, the Guggenheim Foundation, Jimmy Obomba and Amnesty International (the Kampala office), Rory Breaker, Kayondo Wahabu, Asiimwe Deborah and Jerry Gerber.

RUINED

PRODUCTION HISTORY

Ruined was originally commissioned by and received its world premiere at the Goodman Theatre in Chicago (Robert Falls, Artistic Director; Roche Schulfer, Executive Director) in November 2008. The production was co-produced by Manhattan Theatre Club (Lynne Meadow, Artistic Director; Barry Grove, Executive Producer). It was directed by Kate Whoriskey; the set design was by Derek McLane, the lighting design was by Peter Kaczorowski, the costume design was by Paul Tazewell, the sound design was by Rob Milburn and Michael Bodeen and the original music was composed by Dominic Kanza; the dramaturg was Tanya Palmer and the production stage manager was Kimberly Osgood. The cast was:

MAMA NADI	Saidah Arrika Ekulona
JOSEPHINE	Cherise Boothe
SOPHIE	Condola Phyleia Rashad
SALIMA	Quincy Tyler Bernstine
CHRISTIAN	Russell Gebert Jones
MR. HARARI	Tom Mardirosian
JEROME KISEMBE/SOLDIER/AID WORKER	Chris Chalk
COMMANDER OSEMBENGA/SOLDIER	Kevin Mambo
FORTUNE/SOLDIER/MINER	Chiké Johnson
SIMON/SOLDIER/MINER	William Jackson Harper
SOLDIER	Simon Shabantu Kashama
SOLDIER	Ali Amin Carter

Ruined made its New York City premiere at Manhattan Theatre Club (Lynne Meadow, Artistic Director; Barry Grove, Executive Director) in February 2009. It was directed by Kate Whoriskey; the set design was by Derek McLane, the lighting design was by Peter Kaczorowski, the costume design was by Paul Tazewell, the sound design was by Rob Milburn and Michael Bodeen and the original music was composed by Dominic Kanza; the production stage manager was Donald Fried, the stage manager was Alison Desantis and the guitarist was Simon Shabantu Kashama. The cast was:

MAMA NADI	Saidah Arrika Ekulona
JOSEPHINE	Cherise Boothe
SOPHIE	Condola Rashad
SALIMA	Quincy Tyler Bernstine
CHRISTIAN	Russell Gebert Jones
MR. HARARI	Tom Mardirosian
JEROME KISEMBE/SOLDIER	Chris Chalk
COMMANDER OSEMBENGA/SOLDIER	Kevin Mambo
FORTUNE/SOLDIER/MINER	Chiké Johnson
SIMON/SOLDIER/MINER/	
AID WORKER	William Jackson Harper
PASCAL/SOLDIER	Ron McBee

CHARACTERS

MAMA NADI	A madam, a businesswoman, attractive, early forties
JOSEPHINE	One of Mama's girls, early twenties
SOPHIE	One of Mama's girls, eighteen
SALIMA	One of Mama's girls, nineteen
CHRISTIAN	A traveling salesman, early forties
MR. HARARI	A Lebanese diamond merchant, early forties
JEROME KISEMBE	A rebel leader
COMMANDER OSEMBENGA	A military leader for the current government
FORTUNE	A Government Soldier, Salima's husband
SIMON	A Government Soldier, Fortune's cousin
LAURENT	A Government Soldier, Osembenga's assistant
REBEL SOLDIERS	
GOVERNMENT SOLDIERS	
AID WORKER	

SETTING

A small mining town. The Democratic Republic of Congo.

ACT ONE

Scene 1

A small mining town. The sounds of the tropical Ituri rain forest. The Democratic Republic of Congo.

A bar, makeshift furniture and a rundown pool table. A lot of effort has gone into making the worn bar cheerful. A stack of plastic washtubs rests in the corner. An old car battery powers the audio system, a covered birdcage sits conspicuously in the corner of the room.

Mama Nadi, early forties, an attractive woman with an arrogant stride and majestic air, watches Christian, early forties, a perpetually cheerful traveling salesman, knock back a Fanta. His good looks have been worn down by hard living on the road. He wears a suit that might have been considered stylish when new, but it's now nearly ten years old, and overly loved.

CHRISTIAN: Ah. Cold. The only cold Fanta in twenty-five kilometers. You don't know how good this tastes.

(Mama flashes a warm flirtatious smile, then pours herself a Primus beer.)

MAMA: And where the hell have you been?

CHRISTIAN: It was no easy task getting here.

MAMA: I've been expecting you for the last three weeks. How am I supposed do business? No soap, no cigarettes, no condoms. Not even a half liter of petrol for the generator.

CHRISTIAN: Why are you picking a fight with me already? I didn't create this damn chaos. Nobody, and I'm telling you, nobody could get through on the main road. Every two kilometers a boy with a Kalashnikov and pockets that need filling. Toll, tax, tariff. They invent reasons to lighten your load.

MAMA: Then why does Mr. Harari always manage to get through?

CHRISTIAN: Mr. Harari doesn't bring you things you need, does he? Mr. Harari has interests that supercede his safety. Me, I still hope to have a family one day. *(Laughs heartily)*

MAMA: And my lipstick?

CHRISTIAN: Your lipstick? Aye! Did you ask me for lipstick?

MAMA: Of course, I did, you idiot!

CHRISTIAN: Look at the way you speak to me, chérie. *Comment est-ce possible?* You should be happy I made it here in one piece.

(Christian produces a tube of lipstick from his pocket.)

Play nice, or I'll give this to Josephine. She knows just how to show her appreciation.

MAMA: Yes, but you always take home a little more than you ask for with Josephine. I hope you know how to use a condom.

(Christian laughs.)

CHRISTIAN: Are you jealous?

MAMA: Leave me alone, you're too predictable. *(Turns away, dismissive)*

CHRISTIAN: Where are you going? Hey, hey what are you doing? *(Teasingly)* Chérie, I know you wanted me to forget, so you could yell at me, but you won't get the pleasure this time.

(Christian taunts her with the lipstick. Mama resists the urge to smile.)

MAMA: Oh shut up and give it to me.

(He passes her the lipstick.)

Thank you, Christian.
CHRISTIAN: I didn't hear you—
MAMA: Don't press your luck. And it better be red.

(Mama grabs a sliver of a broken mirror from behind the rough-hewn bar, and gracefully applies the lipstick.)

CHRISTIAN: You don't have to say it. I know you want a husband.
MAMA: Like a hole in my head.
CHRISTIAN *(Reciting)*:

> What, is this love?
> An unexpected wind,
> A fluctuation,
> Fronting the coming of a storm.
> Resolve, a thorny bush
> Blown asunder and swept away.

There, chérie. I give you a poem in lieu of the kiss you won't allow me.

(Christian laughs, warmly. Mama puts out a bowl of peanuts, a peace offering.)

MAMA: Here. I saved you some groundnuts, professor.
CHRISTIAN: That's all you saved for me?
MAMA: Be smart, and I'll show you the door in one second.

(Mama scolds him with her eyes.)

CHRISTIAN: Ach, ach . . . why are you wearing my grandmama's face?

(Christian mocks her expression. Mama laughs and downs her beer.)

MAMA: You sure you don't want a beer?
CHRISTIAN: You know me better than that, chérie, I haven't had a drop of liquor in four years.
MAMA *(Teasing)*: It's cold.
CHRISTIAN: Tst!

(Christian cracks open a few peanuts, and playfully pops them into his mouth.
   The parrot squawks.)

What's there? In the cage?
MAMA: Oh, that, a gray parrot. Old Papa Batunga passed.
CHRISTIAN: When?
MAMA: Last Thursday. No one wanted the damn bird. It complains too much.
CHRISTIAN *(Amused)*: Yeah, what does it say?

(Christian walks to the birdcage, and peers under the covering.)

MAMA: Who the hell knows. It speaks pygmy. Old Papa was the last of his tribe. That stupid bird was the only thing he had left to talk to.
CHRISTIAN *(To the bird)*: Hello?
MAMA: He believed as long as the words of the forest people were spoken, the spirits would stay alive.
CHRISTIAN: For true?
MAMA: Yeah, well, when that bird dies this place is gonna lose part of its story.
CHRISTIAN *(Poking his finger into the cage)*: What are you going to do with him?
MAMA: Sell it. I don't want it. It stinks.

CHRISTIAN *(Still poking; to the parrot)*: Hello.

MAMA: Hey, hey don't put your fingers in there.

CHRISTIAN: Look. He likes me. So, Mama, you haven't asked me what else I've brought for you? Go see. *(Quickly withdraws his finger)* Ow. Shit. He bit me.

MAMA: Well, you shouldn't be messing with it. *(Laughs)*

CHRISTIAN: Ow, damn it.

MAMA *(Impatiently)*: Don't be a cry baby, what did you bring me? Well? . . . Are you going to keep me guessing?

CHRISTIAN *(Sitting back down)*: Go on. Take a peek in the truck. And don't say I don't think about you.

MAMA *(Smiling)*: How many?

CHRISTIAN: Three.

MAMA: Three? But, I can't use three right now. You know that.

CHRISTIAN: Of course you can. And I'll give you a good price if you take all of them.

(Mama goes to the doorway, and peers out at the offerings, unimpressed.)

MAMA: I don't know. They look used. Worn.

CHRISTIAN: C'mon, Mama. Take another look. A full look. You've said it yourself business is good.

(Mama considers, then finally:)

MAMA: Okay, one. That one in front. *(Points into the distance)*

CHRISTIAN: Three. C'mon, don't make me travel back with them.

MAMA: Just one. How much?

CHRISTIAN: Do you know how difficult it was getting here? The road was completely washed out—

MAMA: All right, all right. I don't need the whole damn saga. Just tell me, how much for the one?

CHRISTIAN: The same as usual plus twenty-five, because . . . because . . . You understand it wasn't easy to get here with the—

MAMA: I'll give you fifteen.

CHRISTIAN: Ahh! Fifteen? No. That's nothing. Twenty-two. C'mon.

MAMA: Twenty. My best offer.

(Christian mulls it over. He's reluctant.)

CHRISTIAN: Aye. Okay. Okay. Damn it. Yes. Yes. But I expect another cold Fanta. One from the bottom this time.

(Christian, defeated, exits. Mama smiles victoriously, and retrieves another soda from the cooler. She reapplies her lipstick for good measure, then counts out her money.

Christian reenters proudly bearing two cartons of Ugandan cigarettes. A moment later two women in ragged clothing step tentatively into the bar: Sophie, a luminous beauty with an air of defiance, and Salima, a sturdy peasant woman whose face betrays a world-weariness. They hold hands. Mama studies the women, then:)

MAMA: I said one. That one.

(Mama points to Sophie.)

CHRISTIAN: It's been a good week, and I'll tell you what, I'll give you two for the price of one. Why not?

MAMA: Are you deaf? No. Tst! I don't need two more mouths to feed and pester me.

(Mama continues to examine each woman.)

CHRISTIAN: Take both. Feed them as one. Please, Mama, I'll throw in the cigarettes for cost.

MAMA: But, I'll only pay for one.

CHRISTIAN: Of course. We agree, why are we arguing?

MAMA *(Yelling)*: Josephine! Josephine! Where is that stupid woman?

(Josephine, a sexy woman in a short western-style miniskirt and high heels appears in the beaded doorway. She surveys the new women with obvious contempt.)

Take them out back. Get them washed and some proper clothing.

JOSEPHINE: *Kuya apa (Beat) sasa.* (Beckons to the women. They reluctantly follow)*

MAMA: Wait.

(Mama gestures to Salima, who clings to Sophie.)

You. Come here.

(Salima doesn't move.)

Come.

(Salima clings to Sophie, then slowly walks toward Mama.)

What's your name?

SALIMA *(Whispers)*: Salima.

MAMA: What?

SALIMA: Salima.

(Mama examines Salima's rough hands.)

MAMA: Rough. *(With disdain)* A digger. We'll have to do something about that.

(Salima yanks her hand away. Mama registers the bold gesture.)

And you, come. *(Sophie walks to Mama)* You're a pretty thing, what's your name?

* Note: Swahili translations appear at the end of the play.

SOPHIE *(Gently)*: Sophie.

MAMA: Do you have a smile?

SOPHIE: Yes.

MAMA: Then let me see it.

(Sophie struggles to find a halfhearted smile.)

Good. Go get washed up.

(A moment.)

JOSEPHINE *(Snaps)*: C'mon, now!

(Salima looks to Sophie. The women follow behind Josephine. Sophie walks with some pain and effort.)

MAMA: Did you at least tell them this time?

CHRISTIAN: Yes. They know and they came willingly.

MAMA: And . . . ?

CHRISTIAN: Salima is from a tiny village. No place really. She was, captured by rebel soldiers, *Mayi-mayi,* the poor thing spent nearly five months in the bush as their concubine.

MAMA: And what of her people?

CHRISTIAN: She says her husband is a farmer. And from what I understand, her village won't have her back. Because . . . But she's a simple girl, she doesn't have much learning, I wouldn't worry about her.

MAMA: And the other?

CHRISTIAN: Sophie. Sophie is . . .

MAMA: Is what?

CHRISTIAN: . . . is . . . ruined.

(A moment.)

MAMA *(Enraged)*: You brought me a girl that's ruined?

CHRISTIAN: She cost you nothing.

MAMA: I paid money for her, not the other one. The other one is plain. I have half a dozen girls like her, I don't need to feed another plain girl.

CHRISTIAN: I know this, okay, don't get worked-up. Sophie is a good girl, she won't trouble you.

MAMA: How do I know that?

CHRISTIAN (*Defensively*): Because I am telling you. She's seen some very bad times.

MAMA: Yeah? And why is that my concern?

CHRISTIAN: Take her on, just for a month. You'll see she's a good girl. Hard worker.

(Mama gestures toward her own genitals.)

MAMA: But damaged, am I right?

CHRISTIAN: Yes . . . Look, militia did ungodly things to the child, took her with . . . a bayonet and then left her for dead. And she was—

MAMA (*Snaps*): I don't need to hear it. Are you done?

CHRISTIAN (*Passionately*): Things are gonna get busy, Mama. All along the road people are talking about how this red dirt is rich with coltan. Suddenly everyone has a shovel, and wants to stake a claim since that boastful pygmy dug up his fortune in the reserve. I guarantee there'll be twice as many miners here by September. And you know all those bastards will be thirsty. So, take her, put her to work for you.

MAMA: And what makes you think I have any use for her?

CHRISTIAN (*Pleads*): The girl cooks, cleans and she sings like an angel. And you . . . you haven't had nice music here since that one, that beauty Camille got the AIDS.

MAMA: No. A girl like this is bad luck. I can't have it. Josephine! Josephine!

CHRISTIAN: And, Mama, she's pretty pretty. She'll keep the miners eyes happy. I promise.

MAMA: Stop it already, no. You're like a hyena. Won't you shut up, now.

(Josephine enters, put upon.)

JOSEPHINE: Yes, Mama.

MAMA: Bring the girl, Sophie, back.

CHRISTIAN: Wait. Give us a minute, Josephine.

(Josephine doesn't move.)

Mama, please. Look, okay, I'm asking you to do me this favor. I've done many things for you over the years. And I don't ask you for a lot in return. Please. The child has no place else to go.

MAMA: I'm sorry, but I'm running a business not a mission. Take her to the sisters in Bunia, let her weave baskets for them. Josephine, why are you standing there like a fool . . . go get the girl.

CHRISTIAN: Wait.

JOSEPHINE *(Annoyed)*: Do you want me to stay or to go?

MAMA *(Snaps)*: Get her!

(Josephine sucks her teeth and exits.)

CHRISTIAN *(With a tinge of resentment)*: Tst! I remembered your lipstick and everything.

MAMA: Don't look at me that way. I open my doors, and tomorrow I'm refugee camp overrun with suffering. Everyone has their hand open since this damned war began. I can't do it. I keep food in the mouths of eight women when half the country's starving, so don't give me shit about taking on one more girl.

CHRISTIAN: Look. Have anything you want off of my truck. Anything! I even have some . . . some Belgian chocolate.

MAMA: You won't let up. Why are you so damn concerned with this girl? Huh?

CHRISTIAN: C'mon, Mama, please.

MAMA: Chocolate. I always ask you for chocolate, and you always tell me it turns in this heat. How many times have you refused me this year. Huh? But, she must be very very important to you. I see that. Do you want to fuck her or something?

(A moment.)

CHRISTIAN: She's my sister's only daughter. Okay? I told my family I'd find a place for her . . . And here at least I know she'll be safe. Fed.

(He stops himself and gulps down his soda.)

And as you know the village isn't a place for a girl who has been . . . ruined. It brings shame, dishonor to the family.
MAMA *(Ironically)*: But it's okay for her to be here, huh? I'm sorry, but, I can't. I don't have room for another broken girl.
CHRISTIAN: She eats like a bird. Nothing.

(Sophie enters.)

SOPHIE: Madame.
MAMA *(Defensively)*: It's "Mademoiselle."

(Mama stares at Sophie, thinking, her resolve slowly softening.)

Come here.

(Sophie walks over to Mama.)

How old are you?

(Sophie meets Mama's eyes.)

SOPHIE: Eighteen.

MAMA: Yeah? Do you have a beau?
SOPHIE: No.

(*Mama's surprised by her haughtiness.*)

MAMA: Are you a student?
SOPHIE: Yes, I was to sit for the university exam.
MAMA: I bet you were good at your studies. Am I right?
SOPHIE: Yes.
MAMA: A *petit bureaucrat* in the making.

(*Sophie shifts with discomfort. Her body aches, tears escape her eyes. Mama uses her skirt to wipe Sophie's eyes.*)

Did they hurt you badly?
SOPHIE (*Whispered*): . . . Yes.
MAMA: I bet they did.

(*Mama studies Sophie. She considers, then decides:*)

Christian, go get me the chocolate.
CHRISTIAN: Does that mean . . . ?
MAMA: I'm doing this for you, cuz you've been good to me. (*Whispers to Christian*) But this is the last time you bring me damaged goods. Understood? It's no good for business.
CHRISTIAN: Thank you. It's the last time. I promise. Thank you.
MAMA (*To Sophie*): You sing?
SOPHIE (*Softly*): Yes.
MAMA: Do you know any popular songs?
SOPHIE: Yes. A few.
CHRISTIAN: Speak up!

(*Christian exits.*)

SOPHIE: Yes, Mad . . . (*Catching herself*) . . . emoiselle.

MAMA: Mama. You do math? Stuff like that?
SOPHIE: Yes, Mama.
MAMA: Good.

(Mama lifts Sophie's chin with her fingers, enviously examining her face.)

Yes, you're very pretty. I can see how that caused you problems. Do you know what kind of place this is?
SOPHIE: Yes, Mama. I think so.
MAMA: Good.

(Mama carefully applies red lipstick to Sophie's mouth.)

Then we have no problems. I expect my girls to be well behaved and clean. That's all. I provide a bed, food and clothing. If things are good, everyone gets a little. If things are bad, then Mama eats first. Am I making myself clear?

(Sophie nods.)

Good. Red is your color.

(Sophie doesn't respond.)

Thank you, Mama.
SOPHIE: Thank you, Mama.

(Mama pours a glass of local home-brewed liquor. She holds it out.)

MAMA: Here. It'll help the pain down below. I know it hurts, because it smells like the rot of meat. So wash good.

(Sophie takes the glass, and slowly drinks the liquor down.)

Don't get too dependent on drink. It'll make you sloppy, and I have no tolerance for sloppiness. Understood?

(Christian, put upon, reenters with a faded, but pretty, box of chocolates.)

CHRISTIAN: Handmade. Imported. *Très bon.* I hope you're impressed. A Belgian shopkeeper in Bunia ordered them. Real particular. I had a hell of a time trying to find these Goddamn chocolates. And then, poof, she's gone. And now I'm stuck with twenty boxes, I tried to pawn them off on Pastor Robbins, but apparently he's on a diet.

(Mama opens the box, surveying the chocolates. She's in seventh heaven. She offers a piece to Sophie, who timidly selects a piece.)

SOPHIE: Merci.

(Mama bites into the chocolate.)

MAMA: Mmm.

CHRISTIAN: Happy? That's what the good life in Belgium tastes like.

MAMA: Caramel. *(Savoring)* Good God, I haven't had caramel in ages. You bastard, you've been holding out on me! Mmm. Smell 'em, the smell reminds me of my mother. She'd take me and my brothers to Kisangani. And she'd buy us each an enormous bag of caramels wrapped in that impossible plastic. You know why? So we wouldn't tell my grandfather about all of the uncles she visited in the big town. She'd sit us on the bank of the river, watching the boats and eating sweaty caramels, while she "visited with uncles." And as long as there were sweets, we didn't breathe a word, not a murmur, to old Papa.

(Sophie eats her chocolate, smiling for the first time. Christian reaches for a chocolate, but Mama quickly slaps his hand away.)

CHRISTIAN: What about me?
MAMA: What about you?
CHRISTIAN: Don't I get one?
MAMA: No!

(This amuses Sophie. She smiles.)

CHRISTIAN: Why are you smiling? You're a lucky girl. You're lucky you have such a good uncle. A lot of men would've left you for dead.

(Sophie's smile disappears.)

MAMA: Never mind him. *(To Christian)* Go already and bring the other stuff in before the vultures steal it!
CHRISTIAN: Sophie. I'm . . . you . . . you be a good girl. Don't make Mama angry.
SOPHIE: I won't Uncle.

(Christian exits, an apology in his posture. Sophie licks her chocolate-covered fingers as the lights fade.)

Scene 2

A month later. The bar. Josephine cranks the generator. Colorful Christmas lights flicker. The generator hums on. Music and lights provide a festive atmosphere. The birdcage rests in the back of the bar. Periodically the bird makes a raucous.

At the bar, drunk and disheveled Rebel Soldiers drain their beers and laugh too loudly. Salima, wearing a shiny gold midriff, a colorful traditional wrap and mismatched yellow heels, shoots pool, doing her best to ignore the occasional lustful leers of the Soldiers.

Jerome Kisembe, the rebel leader dressed in military uniform, holds court. Mama, toting bowls of peanuts, wears a bright red kerchief around her neck, in recognition of the rebel leader's colors. Josephine dirty-dances for Mr. Harari, a tipsy Lebanese diamond merchant, who sports surprisingly pristine clothing. He is barefoot.

Sophie plows through an upbeat dance song, accompanied by a guitar and drums.

SOPHIE *(Sings)*:
>The liquid night slowly pours in
>Languor peels away like a curtain
>Spirits rise and tongues loosen
>And the weary ask to be forgiven.
>You come here to forget,
>You say drive away all regret
>And dance like it's the ending
>The ending of the war.
>The day's heavy door closes quick
>Leaving the scold of the sun behind
>Dusk ushers in the forest's music
>And your body's free to unwind.

(Josephine dances for the men. They give her tips.)

>You come here to forget,
>You say drive away all regret
>And dance like it's the ending
>The ending of the war.
>But can the music be all forgiving
>Purge the wear and tear of the living?
>Will the sound drown out your sorrow,
>So you'll remember nothing tomorrow?

(A drunk Rebel Soldier stands, and demands attention.)

REBEL SOLDIER #1: Another! Hey!

MAMA: I hear you! I hear you!

REBEL SOLDIER #1: C'mon! Another!

(He clumsily slams the bottle on the counter. He gestures to Sophie.)

Psst! You! Psst! Psst!

(Another Rebel Soldier gives Sophie a catcall. Sophie ignores him. Rebel Soldier #1 turns his attention back to Mama.)

Her! Why won't she come talk to me?

MAMA: You want to talk to her. Behave, and let me see your money.

(Kisembe, haughty, lets out a roar of a laugh.)

REBEL SOLDIER #1: The damn beer drained my pocket. It cost too much! You're a fucking thief!

MAMA: Then go somewhere else. And mind your tongue. *(Turns away)*

REBEL SOLDIER #1: Hey. Wait. Wait. I want her to talk to me. Mama, lookie! I have this. *(Proudly displays a cloth filled with little chunks of ore)*

MAMA: What is it? Huh? Coltan? Where'd you get it?

REBEL SOLDIER #1 *(Boasting)*: From a miner on the reserve.

MAMA: He just gave it to you?

REBEL SOLDIER #1 *(Snickering)*: Yeah, he give it to me. Dirty poacher been diggin' up our forest, we run 'em off. Run them good, gangsta style: "Muthafucka run!" Left 'em for the fucking scavengers.

(The Rebel Soldier strikes a hip-hop "gangsta-style" pose. The other Soldiers laugh. Mr. Harari, unamused, ever so slightly registers the conversation. Mama laughs.)

MAMA: Coltan? Let me see. Ah, that's nothing, it's worthless my friend. A month ago, yes, but now you can't get a handful of meal for it. Too many prospectors. Every miner that walks in here has a bucket of it. Bring me a gram of gold, then we talk.

REBEL SOLDIER #1: What do you mean? Liar! In the city, this would fetch me plenty.

MAMA: This ain't the city, is it, Soldier?

(He aggressively grabs Mama's wrist.)

This is a nice place for a drink. Yeah? I don't abide by bush laws. If you want to drink like a man, you drink like a man. You want to behave like gorilla, then go back into the bush.

(The Soldiers laugh. The Rebel Soldier unhands Mama.)

REBEL SOLDIER #1: C'mon, Mama, this is worth plenty! Yeah?

(Again, he gestures to Sophie. He's growing increasingly belligerent.)

Bitch. Why won't she talk to me?

(Frustrated, he puts the cloth back in his pocket. He broods, silently watching Sophie sway to the music. Then all of a sudden he collects himself, and drunkenly makes his way toward her.)

I'll teach her manners! Respect me!

(He pounds his chest, another Soldier goads him on. Sophie stiffens. The music stops. Mama quickly steps between them.)

MAMA: But . . . as the coltan is all you have. I'll take it this time. Now go sit down. Sit down. Please.

REBEL SOLDIER #1 (*Excited*): Yeah? Now, I want her to talk to me! Will she talk to me?

MAMA: Okay. Okay. Sit.

(*He pulls out the cloth again. He gently removes several pieces of the ore.*)

Don't be stingy. Tst! Let me see all of it.

(*He reluctantly relinquishes the weathered cloth to Mama.*)

(*Smiling*) Salima! Salima, come!

(*Salima bristles at the sound of her name. She reluctantly approaches the Soldier. Mama shows her off to him.*)

REBEL SOLDIER #1: What about her? (*Gestures to Sophie*)

MAMA: Salima is better dancer. (*Salima dances, seductively*) I promise. Okay. Everyone is happy.

KISEMBE: Soldier, everyone is happy!

(*Salima sizes up the drunken Soldier.*)

SALIMA: So, "Gangsta," you wanna dance with me?

(*She places his arms around her waist. He longingly looks over at Sophie, then pulls Salima close. He leads aggressively.*)

Easy.

MAMA: Sophie.

(*Sophie, relieved, resumes singing. Salima and the Rebel Soldier dance.*)

SOPHIE (*Sings*):
       Have another beer, my friend,
       Douse the fire of your fears, my friend,
       Get drunk and foolish on the moment,

Brush aside the day's heavy judgment.
Yes, have another beer, my friend,
Wipe away the angry tears, my friend,
Get drunk and foolish on the moment,
Brush aside the day's heavy judgment.
Cuz you come here to forget,
You say drive away all regret,
And dance like it's the ending
The ending of the war.
The ending of the war.
The ending of the war.

(*Applause. Mr. Harari tips Sophie. Mama having quenched the fire, fetches her lockbox from a hiding place beneath the counter, and puts the ore inside.*)

MR. HARARI: That one, she's pretty. (*Gestures to Sophie*)
JOSEPHINE (*With disdain*): Sophie?! She's broken. All of the girls think she's bad luck.

(*Josephine leads Mr. Harari to the table. He sits.*)

MR. HARARI: What are you wearing? Where's the dress I bought you?
JOSEPHINE: If I had known you were coming, I'd have put it on.
MR. HARARI: Then what are you waiting for, my darling?

(*Josephine exits quickly. Mama, toting her lockbox, joins Mr. Harari at his table.*)

MAMA: What happened to your shoes, Mr. Harari?
MR. HARARI: Your fucking country, some drunk child doing his best impersonation of a rebel soldier liberated my shoes. Every time I come here I have to buy a new fucking pair of shoes.

(Laughter from the pool table.)

MAMA: You're lucky he only wanted your shoes. *Sante.*

(The Soldier gets too friendly with Salima. She lurches away, and falls against the pool table.)

REBEL SOLDIER #1: Hey!
KISEMBE: Ach, ach, behave, I'm trying to play here.

(The Solider grabs Salima onto his lap. Mr. Harari weighs the situation.)

MR. HARARI *(To Mama)*: You took that poor man's coltan. Shame on you. He probably doesn't know what he gave away for the taste of that woman. *(To Soldier)* Savor it! The toll to enter that tunnel was very expensive, my friend. *(To Mama)* We both know how much it would fetch on the market.
MAMA: Yeah, so? Six months ago it was just more black dirt. I don't get why everyone's crawling over each other for it.
MR. HARARI: Well, my darling, in this damnable age of the mobile phone it's become quite the precious ore, no? And for what ever reason, God has seen fit to bless your back-ward country with an abundance of it. Now, if that young man had come to me, I would've given him enough money to buy pussy for a month. Even yours. So who's the big-ger thief, you or him?
MAMA: He give it to me, you saw. So, does that make me a thief or merely more clever than you.

(Mr. Harari laughs.)

MR. HARARI: My darling, you'd do well in Kisangani.
MAMA: I do well here, and I'd get homesick in Kisangani. It's a filthy city full of bureaucrats and thieves.

MR. HARARI: Very funny, but I imagine you'd enjoy it, terribly.
    And I mean that as a compliment.
MAMA: Do you have a minute?
MR. HARARI: Of course.
KISEMBE: Soldier! Soldier!
REBEL SOLDIER #2: Chief.
KISEMBE: Bring me my mobile! What're you, an old man? Hurry!

(Mama empties a bag containing stones onto a cloth on the table.)

MAMA: What do you think? Huh?
MR. HARARI *(Referring to the diamonds)*: Just looking, I can tell
    you, most of these are worthless. I'm sorry.

(Mama takes out another stone, and places it on the table.)

MAMA: What about that one?

(Mama points to the rough stone. Mr. Harari examines the diamond on the table, then meticulously places a loup to his eye and examines it. He looks over his shoulder.)

MR. HARARI *(Whispers)*: Hm. It's a raw diamond. Where'd you
    get this?
MAMA: Don't you worry. I'm holding it for someone.
MR. HARARI *(Continues to examine the diamond)*: Nice. Yes, you
    see, there. It carries the light well.
MAMA: Yeah, yeah, but is it worth anything?
MR. HARARI: Well . . .
MAMA: Well . . .
MR. HARARI: Depends.

(Mama smiles.)

It's raw, and the market—

MAMA: Yeah, yeah, but, what are we talking? Huh? A new generator or a plot of land?

MR. HARARI (*Chuckling*): Slow down, I can offer you a fairly good price. But, be reasonable, darling, I'm an independent with a family that doesn't appreciate how hard I work.

(*Mama takes back the diamond.*)

MAMA: You sound like old Papa. He was like you, Mr. Harari, work too much, always want more, no rest. When there was famine his bananas were rotting. He used to say as long as the forest grows a man will never starve.

MR. HARARI: Does he still have his farm?

MAMA (*Smiling to herself*): You know better, Mr. Harari, you're in the Congo. Things slip from our fingers like butter. No. When I was eleven, this white man with skin the color of wild berries turned up with a piece of paper. It say he have rights to my family land. (*With acid*) Just like that. Taken! And you want to hear a joke? Poor old Papa bought magic from a friend, he thought a handful of powder would give him back his land. (*Examining the diamond*) Everyone talk talk diamonds, but I . . . I want a powerful slip of paper that says I can cut down forests and dig holes and build to the moon if I choose. I don't want someone to turn up at my door, and take my life from me. Not ever again. But tell, how does a woman like me get a piece of land, without having to pick up a fucking gun?

(*Mr. Harari cautiously watches the Rebel Soldiers.*)

MR. HARARI: These, these idiots keep changing the damn rules on us. You file papers, and the next day the office is burned down. You buy land, and the next day the chief's son has built a fucking house on it. I don't know why anybody bothers. Madness. And look at them. (*Gestures to the Rebel Soldiers*) A hungry pygmy digs a hole in the forest, and suddenly every two-bit militia is battling for the keys to hell.

MAMA: True, chérie, but someone must provide them with beer and distractions.

(Mr. Harari laughs. Mama scoops up the stones and places them back into her lockbox.)

MR. HARARI: Just, be careful, where will I drink if anything happens to you?

(Mr. Harari gives Mama a friendly kiss.)

MAMA: Don't worry about me. Everything is beautiful.

(Josephine enters proudly sporting an elegant traditional dress.)

JOSEPHINE: What do you think?

(Mr. Harari shifts his gaze to Josephine.)

MR. HARARI: Such loveliness. Doesn't she look beautiful?
MAMA: Yes, very. *Karibu.*
MR. HARARI: I just might have to take you home with me.
JOSEPHINE *(Excited)*: Promise.
MR. HARARI: Of course.

(Josephine hitches up her dress and straddles Mr. Harari. She kisses him.)

KISEMBE *(Shouts)*: Mama! Mama!
MAMA: Okay, okay, chief, *sawa sawa.*
KISEMBE: Two more Primus. And, Mama, why can't I get mobile service in this pit?
MAMA: You tell me, you're important, go make it happen!

MR. HARARI: Who's that?

JOSEPHINE: Him? Jerome Kisembe, leader of the rebel militia. He's very powerful. He have sorcerer that give him a charm so he can't be touched by bullet. He's fearless. He is the boss man, the government and the church and anything else he wants to be.

(Mr. Harari studies Kisembe.)

Don't look so hard at a man like that.

(Josephine grabs Mr. Harari's face and kisses him. Mama clears the beer bottles from Kisembe's table. The Soldier gropes at Salima, he nips her on the neck.)

SALIMA: Ow! You jackass.

(Salima pulls away from the Soldier and heads for the door. Mama races after her, catching her arm forcefully.)

MAMA: What's your problem?

SALIMA: Did you see what he did?

MAMA: You selfish girl. Now get back to him.

(Mama shoves Salima back toward the Soldier. Sophie, watching, runs over to Salima.)

SOPHIE: Are you all right, Salima?

SALIMA: The dog bit me. (Whispered) I'm not going back over there.

SOPHIE: You have to.

SALIMA: He's filth! It's a man like him that—

SOPHIE: Don't. Mama's looking.

SALIMA (Tears welling up in her eyes): Do you know what he said to me—

SOPHIE: They'll say anything to impress a lady. Half of them are lies. Dirty fucking lies! Go back, don't listen. I'll sing the song you like.

(Sophie gives Salima a kiss on the cheek. Salima's eyes shoot daggers at Mama, but she reluctantly returns to the drunken Soldier. Sophie launches into another song. Josephine dirty-dances for Mr. Harari.)

> Have another beer, my friend,
> Wipe away the angry tears, my friend,
> Get drunk and foolish on the moment,
> Brush aside the day's heavy judgment.
> Cuz you come here to forget,
> You say drive away all regret
> And dance like it's the ending
> And dance like it's the ending

(The music crescendos.)

> The ending
> The ending
> The ending
> And dance like it's the ending . . .

(Mama watches Salima like a hawk. The lights fade.)

Scene 3

Morning. Living quarters behind the bar. Ragged wood-and-straw beds. A poster of a popular African American pop star hangs over Josephine's bed. Sophie paints Salima's fingernails, as she peruses a worn fashion magazine. Salima shifts in place, agitated.

SALIMA (Impatiently): C'mon, c'mon, c'mon, Sophie. Finish before she comes back.

SOPHIE: Keep still, will ya. Stop moving. She's with Mr. Harari.

SALIMA: She's gonna kill me if she find out I use her nail polish.

SOPHIE: Well, keep it up, and she's gonna find out one of these days.

SALIMA: But, not today. So hurry!

(Sophie makes a mistake with Salima's nails. Salima violently yanks her hand away.)

Aye girl, look what you did! *Pumbafu!*

SOPHIE: What's your problem?!

SALIMA: Nothing. Nothing. I'm fine.

(Salima, frustrated, stands up and walks away.)

SOPHIE: Yeah? You've been short with me all morning? Don't turn away. I'm talking to you.

SALIMA: "Smile, Salima. Talk pretty." Them soldiers don't respect nothing. Them miners, they easy, they want drink, company, and it's over. But the soldiers, they want more of you, and—

SOPHIE: Did that man do something to hurt you?

SALIMA: You know what he say? He say fifteen Hema men were shot dead and buried in their own mining pit, in mud so thick it swallow them right into the ground without mercy. He say, one man stuff the coltan into his mouth to keep the soldiers from stealing his hard work, and they split his belly open with a machete. "It'll show him for stealing," he say, bragging like I should be congratulating him. And then he fucked me, and when he was finished he sat on the floor and wept. He wanted me to hold him. Comfort him.

SOPHIE: And, did you?

SALIMA: No. I'm Hema. One of those men could be my brother.

SOPHIE: Don't even say that.

(Salima is overcome by the possibility.)

SALIMA: I . . . I . . . miss my family. My husband. My baby—

SOPHIE: Stop it! We said we wouldn't talk about it.

SALIMA: This morning I was thinking about Beatrice and how much she liked banana. I feed her like this. I squeeze banana between my fingers and let her suck them, and she'd make a funny little face. Such delight. Delight. *(Emotionally)* Delight! Delight!

SOPHIE: Shhh! Lower your voice.

SALIMA: Please, let me say my baby's name, Beatrice.

SOPHIE: Shhh!

SALIMA: I wanna go home!

SOPHIE: Now, look at me. Look here, if you leave, where will you go? Huh? Sleep in the bush? Scrounge for food in a stinking refugee camp.

SALIMA: But I wanna—!

SOPHIE: What? Be thrown back out there? Where will you go? Huh? Your husband? Your village? How much goodness did they show you?

SALIMA *(Wounded)*: Why did you say that?

SOPHIE: I'm sorry, but you know it's true. There is a war going on, and it isn't safe for a woman alone. You know that! It's better this way. Here.

SALIMA: You, you don't have to be with them. Sometimes their hands are so full of rage that it hurts to be touched. This night, I look over at you singing, and you seem almost happy like a sunbird that can fly away if you reach out to touch it.

SOPHIE: Is that what you think? While I'm singing, I'm praying the pain will be gone, but what those men did to me lives inside of my body. Every step I take I feel them in me. Punishing me. And it will be that way for the rest of my life.

(Salima touches Sophie's face.)

SALIMA: I'm pregnant.

SOPHIE: What?

SALIMA: I'm pregnant. I can't tell Mama. *(Tears fill her eyes)*

(Sophie hugs Salima.)

SOPHIE: No. Shh. Shh. Okay. Okay.

SALIMA: She'll turn me out.

(Sophie breaks away from Salima and digs in a basket for a book.)

What are you doing?

SOPHIE: Shh. Look, look.

(Sophie pulls money from between the pages of the book and empties the bills onto the bed.)

SALIMA: Sophie?!

SOPHIE: Shhh. This is for us. We won't be here forever. Okay.

SALIMA: Where'd you get . . . the money?

SOPHIE: Don't worry. Mama may be many things, but she don't count so good. And when there's enough we'll get a bus to Bunia. I promise. But you can't say anything, not even to Josephine. Okay?

SALIMA: But if Mama finds out that you're—

SOPHIE: Shhhh. She won't.

(Josephine, bedraggled, enters and throws herself on the bed.)

JOSEPHINE: What you two whispering about?

SOPHIE: Nothing.

(Sophie hides the nail polish and book beneath the mattress.)

JOSEPHINE: God, I'm starving. And there's never anything to eat. I thought you were going to save me some fufu.

SOPHIE: I did, I put it on the shelf under the cloth.

SALIMA: I bet that stupid monkey took it again. Pesky creature.

JOSEPHINE: It ain't the monkey, it's Emeline's nasty child. He's a menace. That boy's buttocks would be raw if he were mine.

(Josephine takes off her shirt, revealing an enormous disfiguring black scar circumventing her stomach. She tries to hide it. Sophie's eyes are drawn to the scar.)

(To Salima) But, if it's you who's been pinching my supper, don't think I won't find out. I ain't the only one who's noticed that you getting fat fat off the same food we eating. *(To Sophie)* What are you looking at? *(Tosses her shirt to Sophie)* Hang up my shirt! *Sasa!*

(Sophie hangs Josephine's shirt on a nail.)

SALIMA: Tst. *(Whispers under her breath)*

JOSEPHINE: And what's wrong with her?

SALIMA: Nothing.

(Josephine suspiciously sniffs the air. Then puts on a traditional colorful wrap. A moment. Salima sits back on the bed. Josephine notices her magazine on the bed.)

JOSEPHINE: Hey, girl, why is my fashion magazine here? Huh?

SALIMA: I . . . I had a quick look.

JOSEPHINE: What do you want with it? Can you even read?

SALIMA: Oh, shut your mouth, I like looking at the photographs.

JOSEPHINE: Oh, c'mon, girl, you've seen them a dozen times. It's the same photographs that were there yesterday.

SALIMA: So why do you care if I look at them?

SOPHIE: *Atsha, makelle.* Let her see it, Josephine. Let's not have the same argument.

JOSEPHINE: There.

SALIMA *(Whispered)*: Bitch.

JOSEPHINE: What?

SALIMA: Thank you.

JOSEPHINE: Yeah, that's what I thought.

(Josephine tosses the magazine at Salima.)

Girl, I really should charge you for all the times your dirty fingers fuss with it. *(Sucks her teeth)*

SOPHIE: Oh, give us peace, she doesn't feel well.

JOSEPHINE: No?

(Salima, moping, thumbs through the magazine, doing her best to ignore Josephine.)

SALIMA: The only reason I don't read is cuz my younger sister get school, and I get good husband.

JOSEPHINE: So where is he?!

(Salima ignores her. Josephine turns on the portable radio hanging over her bed.)

ANNOUNCER *(Voice-over)*: *Nous avons reçu des rapports que les bandits armés de Lendu et des groupes rivaux de Hema combattent pour la commande de la ville—*

SALIMA: What's he say?

SOPHIE: Lendu and Hema, fighting near Bunia.

(Josephine quickly turns the radio dial. Congolese hip-hop music plays. She does a few quick suggestive steps, then lights a cigarette.)

JOSEPHINE: Hey. Hey. Guess what? Guess what? I'm going to Kisangani next month.

SOPHIE: What?

JOSEPHINE: Mr. Harari is going to take me. Watch out, chérie, he's promised to set me up in a high-rise apartment. Don't hate, all of this fineness belongs in the city.

SOPHIE: For true?

JOSEPHINE: What, you think I'm lying?

SOPHIE: No, no, that's real cool, Josephine. The big town. You been?

JOSEPHINE: Me? . . . No. No. *(To Salima)* And I know you haven't.

SALIMA: How do you know? Huh? I was planning to go some time next year. My husband—

JOSEPHINE *(Sarcastically)*: What, he was going to sell his yams in the market?

SALIMA: I'll ask you not to mention my family.

JOSEPHINE: And if I do?

SALIMA: I'm asking you kindly this time.

(Josephine recognizes the weight of her words but forges on.)

JOSEPHINE: I'm tired of hearing about your family. *(Blows smoke at Salima)*

SALIMA: Mention them again, and I swear to God I'll beat your ass.

JOSEPHINE: Yeah?

SALIMA: Yeah. You don't know what the hell you're talking about.

JOSEPHINE: I don't? All right. I'm stupid! I don't! You are smarter than all of us. Yeah? That's what you think, huh? *Kiwele wele.* You wait, girl. I'll forgive you, I will, when you say, "Josephine you were so so right."

SOPHIE: Just shut up!

JOSEPHINE: Hey, I'm done.

(Josephine blows a kiss. Salima, enraged, starts for the door.)

SOPHIE: Salima, Salima.

(Salima is gone.)

JOSEPHINE *(Taunting)*: Salima!

(Josephine falls on the bed laughing.)

SOPHIE: What's wrong with you? What did Salima do to you?
You make me sick. *(Flicks off the radio)*
JOSEPHINE: Hey, *jolie fille. (Makes kissing sounds)*
SOPHIE: Don't talk to me.
JOSEPHINE: I can't talk to you? Who put you on the top shelf?
You flutter about here as if God touched only you. What
you seem to forget is that this is a whorehouse, chérie.
SOPHIE: Yeah, but, I'm not a whore.
JOSEPHINE: A mere trick of fate. I'm sorry, but let me say what
we all know, you are something worse than a whore. So
many men have had you that you're worthless.

(A moment. Sophie, wounded, turns and limps away silently.)

Am I wrong?
SOPHIE: . . . Yes.
JOSEPHINE: Am I wrong?
SOPHIE: Yes.
JOSEPHINE: My father was chief!

(Sophie is at the door. Josephine confronts her.)

My father was chief! The most important man in my village, and when the soldiers raided us, who was kind to
me? Huh? Not his second wife: "There! She is the chief's
daughter!" Or the cowards who pretended not to know
me. And did any of them bring a blanket to cover me, did
anyone move to help me? NO! So you see, you ain't special!

(The lights fade.)

Scene 4

Dusk. The generator hums. Sophie sings. The bar bustles with activity: Miners, Prostitutes, Musicians and Government Soldiers. Laughter. A Miner chats up Salima. Josephine sits at a table with a Soldier.

SOPHIE *(Sings)*:

>A rare bird on a limb
>Sings a song heard by a few,
>A few patient and distant listeners
>Hear, its sweet sweet call,
>A sound that haunts the forest,
>A cry that tells a story, harmonious,
>But time forgotten.
>To be seen, is to be doomed
>It must evade, evade capture,
>And yet the bird
>Still cries out to be heard.
>And yet the bird
>Still cries out to be heard.
>And yet the bird
>Still cries out to be heard.

(Mama enters. She feeds the parrot.)

MAMA: Hello. Talk to me. You hungry? Yes?
CHRISTIAN *(Entering)*: Mama!

(Mama is surprised by Christian. Her face lights up.)

MAMA: Ah, professor!

(Mama cracks open a couple of sodas. Christian places a box of chocolates and several cartons of cigarettes on the counter then launches into a poem:)

CHRISTIAN:

> The tidal dance,
> A nasty tug of war,
> Two equally implacable partners
> Day fighting night . . .

And so forth and so on. Forgive me, I bring you an early poem, but I'm afraid it's running away from my memory. I still hope one day you will hear the music and dance with me.

MAMA *(Dismissive)*: You're a ridiculous man.

(Mama passes a cold soda to Christian. He blows a kiss to Sophie.)

CHRISTIAN: Lovely, chérie. It's what I've been waiting for.

MAMA: You're the only man I know who doesn't crave a cold beer at the end of a long drive.

CHRISTIAN: Last time I had a drink, I lost several years of my life.

(Mama hands him a list.)

What's this?

MAMA: A list of everything I know you forgot to bring me.

(Christian examines the list.)

CHRISTIAN: What? When'd you learn to spell so good?

MAMA: Oh, close your mouth. Sophie wrote it down. She's a smart girl, been helping me.

CHRISTIAN *(Teasing)*: You see how things work out. And you, you wanted to turn her away—

MAMA: Are you finished?

(Salima and the Miner laugh and play pool.)

I looked out for you on Friday. What the hell happened?

CHRISTIAN: I had to deliver supplies to the mission. Have you heard? Pastor Robbins been missing for a couple days.

(*The Soldier whispers something in Josephine's ear. She laughs loudly, flirtatiously.*)

I told them I'd ask about.

MAMA: The white preacher? I'm not surprised. He's gotta big fucking mouth. The mission's better off without him. The only thing that old bastard ever did was pass out flaky aspirin and maybe a round of penicillin if you were dying.

CHRISTIAN: Well, the rumor is the pastor's been treating wounded rebel soldiers.

MAMA (*Concerned*): Really?

CHRISTIAN: That's what I'm hearing. Things are getting ugly over that way.

MAMA: Since when?

CHRISTIAN: Last week or so. The militias, they're battling for control of the area. It is impossible.

MAMA: What about Yaka-yaka mine? Has the fighting scared off the miners?

CHRISTIAN: I don't know about the miners, but it's scaring me.

(*Salima and the Miner laugh.*)

I was just by Yaka-yaka. When I was there six months ago, it was a forest filled with noisy birds, now it looks like God spooned out heaping mouthfuls of earth, and every stupid bastard is trying to get a taste of it. It's been ugly, chérie, but never like this. Not here.

MAMA: No more talk.

(*She's spooked, but doesn't want to show it. She signals for the Musicians to play an upbeat song. The song plays softly.*)

There will always be squabbles, ancient and otherwise.

(Josephine takes the Soldier to the back.)

Me, I thank God for deep dirty holes like Yaka-yaka. In my house I try to keep everyone happy.

CHRISTIAN: Don't fool yourself!

MAMA: Hey, hey, professor, are you worried about me?

CHRISTIAN *(Gently taking Mama's hand)*: Of course, chérie. I am a family man at heart. A lover, baby. We could build a nice business together. I have friends in Kampala, I have friends in Bamako, I even have friends in Paris, the city of love.

(Mama laughs. She quickly withdraws her hand from Christian. His affection throws her off-balance.)

MAMA: You ... are ... a stupid ... man ... with a running tongue. And look here, I have my own business, and I'm not leaving it for a jackass who doesn't have enough sense to buy a new suit.

CHRISTIAN: You are too proud and stubborn, you know that. This is a good suit, *très chic*, so what if it's old? And ... don't pretend, chérie, eventually you'll grace me with ... a dance.

MAMA: Oh, have a cold beer, it'll flush out some of your foolishness.

CHRISTIAN: Ach, ach, woman! Liquor is not a dance partner I choose.

(Christian does a few seductive dance steps, just then Commander Osembenga, a pompous peacock of a man in dark sunglasses, a gold chain and a jogging suit, struts into the bar. He wears a pistol in a harness. He is accompanied by a Government Soldier in uniform. Christian nods deferentially.)

Monsieur.

*(Osembenga stands erect waiting to be acknowledged. Every-
one grows silent.)*

MAMA *(Flirtatiously)*: Good evening.
OSEMBENGA: It is now.

(He gives the place a once-over.)

MAMA: Can I get you something?
OSEMBENGA: Bring me a cold Primus. A pack of cigarettes, fresh.

*(Mama guides Osembenga to a chair. She signals Sophie to
fetch some beer.)*

MAMA: Monsieur, I must ask you to leave your bullets at the bar,
otherwise you don't come in.
OSEMBENGA: And if I choose not to.
MAMA: Then you don't get served. I don't want any mischief in
here. Is that clear?

*(Osembenga, charmed by her tenacity, laughs with the robust
authority of a man in charge.)*

OSEMBENGA: Do you know who I am?
MAMA: I'm afraid you must edify me, and then forgive me, if it
makes absolutely no difference. Once you step through my
door, then you're in my house. And I make the rules here.

(Osembenga chuckles to himself.)

OSEMBENGA: All right, Mama. Forgive me.

*(Osembenga makes a show of removing the bullets from his
gun and placing them on the table.)*

And who said I don't respect the rule of law?

(The drunk Government Soldier, half dressed, playfully chases Josephine from the back. Josephine spots Osembenga and jumps to attention.)

GOVERNMENT SOLDIER #1: Commander, beg my pardon.
OSEMBENGA: Take it easy, young man. Take it easy. We're all off
duty. We're in Mama's house. Clean up.

(Osembenga sits down. He unzips his jacket. Mama opens a pack of cigarettes and passes them to Osembenga.)

MAMA: Monsieur, I don't recall seeing you here before.
OSEMBENGA: No.

(Mama lights Osembenga's cigarette.)

MAMA: What brings you to mon hotel?
OSEMBENGA: Jerome Kisembe, the rebel leader.

(Osembenga studies her face to gauge the response.)

You know him, of course.
MAMA: I know of him. We all know of him. His name is spoken
here at least several times a day. We've felt the sting of his
reputation.
OSEMBENGA: So, you do know him.
MAMA: No, as I said, I know of him. His men control the road
east and the forest to the north of here.

(Osembenga turns his attention to everyone. Scrutiny. Suspicion.)

OSEMBENGA: Is that so?
MAMA: Yes. But you must know that.

(Osembenga speaks to Mama, but he is clearly addressing everyone.)

OSEMBENGA: This Jerome Kisembe is a dangerous man. You hide him and his band of renegades in your villages. Give them food, and say you're protecting your liberator. What liberator? What will he give the people? That is what I want to know? What has he given you Mama? Hm? A new roof? Food? Peace?

MAMA: I don't need a man to give me anything

OSEMBENGA: Make a joke, but Kisembe has one goal and that is to make himself rich on your back, Mama.

(Osembenga grows loud and more forthright as he speaks. The music stops. The bar grows quiet. Tension.)

He will burn your crops, steal your women, and make slaves of your men all in the name of peace and reconciliation. Don't believe him. He, and men like him, these careless militias wage a diabolical campaign. They leave stains everywhere they go. And remember the land he claims as his own, it is a national reserve, it is the people's land, our land. And yet he will tell you the government has taken everything, though we're actually paving the way for democracy.

MAMA: I know that, but the government needs to let him know that. But you, I'm only seeing you for the first time. Kisembe, I hear his name every day.

OSEMBENGA: Then hear my name, Commander Osembenga, *banga liwa.*

(A moment. Mama absorbs the news, she seems genuinely humbled. Christian backs away as if to disappear.)

You will hear my name quite a bit from now on.

MAMA: Commander Osembenga, forgive me for not knowing your name. *Karibu.* It's a pleasure to have such an important man in our company. Allow me to pour you a glass of our very best whiskey. From the U.S. of A.

Thomas. O. Ott

(1) F - 1923, 089

The Italian Revolution

(2) F. 1923. D 83 2005

773.50	75,765.43
	95,765.43
200.00	95,565.43
	125,565.43
200.00	125,365.43
	144,665.43
309.40	144,356.03
386.75	143,969.28
464.10	143,505.18
618.80	142,886.38
510.51	142,375.87
773.50	141,602.37
1,452.58	140,149.79
301.77	139,848.02
3,000.00	136,848.02
2,500.00	134,348.02
30,000.00	104,348.02
10,000.00	94,348.02
2,000.00	92,348.02
69,551.98	92,348.02
	0.00
6,000.00	-6,000.00
10,000.00	-16,000.00
	1,300.00
11,300.00	-10,000.00
10,000.00	-20,000.00
	30,300.00
40,300.00	-10,000.00
20,000.00	-30,000.00
30,000.00	-60,000.00
	-30,700.00
19,300.00	-50,000.00
146,900.00	-50,000.00

OSEMBENGA: Thank you. A clean glass.

MAMA: Of course. *Karibu.*

(Mama fetches Osembenga a glass of whiskey. She makes a show of wiping out the cloudy glass. She pours him a generous glass of whiskey and places the bottle in front of him.)

(Seductively) We take good care of our visitors. And we offer very good company. Clean company, not like other places. You are safe here. If you need something, anything while—

OSEMBENGA: You are a practical woman. I know that you have the sense to keep your doors closed to rebel dogs. Am I right?

(Osembenga gently takes Mama's hand. She allows the intimacy. Christian looks on. Contempt.)

MAMA: Of course.

(A Miner, covered in mud, sneaks in.)

Hey, hey, my friend. Wash your hands and feet in the bucket outside!

(The Miner, annoyed, scrambles out of the bar.)

These fucking miners have no respect for nothing. I have to tell that one every time.

(Christian retreats to the bar, fuming. Osembenga takes note of him. Christian quickly averts his gaze.)

(Obsequiously) Anything you need.

OSEMBENGA: I will keep that in mind.

MAMA: Ladies.

(She beckons to Josephine and Salima, who join Osembenga at the table. The Government Soldiers groan.)

JOSEPHINE: Commander.

(Josephine places her hand on Osembenga's thigh.)

MAMA: Excuse me a moment.

(Christian grabs Mama's arm as she passes.)

CHRISTIAN: Watch that one.
MAMA: What? It's always good to have friends in the government, no?

(Mama clears bottles. The Miner reenters. He sits at the bar.)

GOVERNMENT SOLDIER #1 *(Abandoned by Josephine, belligerently)*: Another.
MAMA: Show me your money.

(The Soldier holds up his money.)

Sophie! Sophie! What are you standing around for? I'm losing money as you speak. Quick. Quick. Two beers.

(Sophie carries two beers over to the Soldier. He places his money on the table. Sophie picks it up and quickly slips it under her shirt. She doesn't realize Mama is watching her. The drunken Soldier grabs her onto his lap. Christian protectively rises. Sophie skillfully extracts herself from the Soldier's lap.)

CHRISTIAN: Are you okay?
SOPHIE: Yes.

(Sophie, shaken, exits. Christian smiles to himself, and lights a cigarette. The drunken Soldier, annoyed, plops down next to Christian.)

GOVERNMENT SOLDIER #1: *Ça va, Papa?*
CHRISTIAN: *Bien merci.*

(The Soldier stares down Christian.)

GOVERNMENT SOLDIER #1: You give me a cigarette, my friend?
CHRISTIAN *(Nervously)*: Sorry, this is my last one.
GOVERNMENT SOLDIER #1: Yeah? You, buy me cigarette?
CHRISTIAN: What?
GOVERNMENT SOLDIER #1 *(Showing off)*: Buy me cigarette!
CHRISTIAN: Sure.

(Christian reluctantly digs into his pocket, and places money on the counter. Mama drops a cigarette on the counter. The Soldier scoops it up triumphantly, and walks away.)

And? Merci?

(The Soldier stops short, and menacingly stares down Christian.)

OSEMBENGA: Soldier, show this good man the bush hasn't robbed you of your manners.

(A moment.)

GOVERNMENT SOLDIER #1: Merci.

(Christian acknowledges Osembenga with a polite nod.)

OSEMBENGA: Of course.

(Osembenga smiles, and gestures to Mama.)

MAMA: Yes, Commander?
OSEMBENGA *(Referring to Christian, whispers)*: Who is he?
MAMA: Passing through.

(The Soldier, embarrassed, angrily drives the Miner out of his bar seat. The Miner retreats.)

OSEMBENGA: What's his business?
MAMA: Salesman. He's nobody.
OSEMBENGA: I don't trust him.
MAMA: Does he look dangerous to you?
OSEMBENGA: Everyone looks dangerous to me, until I've shared a drink with them.

(Osembenga sizes up Christian, deciding.)

Give him a glass of whiskey, and tell him I hope he finds success here.

(Mama pours a glass of whiskey. She walks over to Christian.)

MAMA: Good news, the commander has bought you a drink of whiskey and hopes that you'll find prosperity.
CHRISTIAN: That's very generous, but you know I don't drink. Please, tell him thanks, but no thanks.

(A moment.)

MAMA: The commander is buying you a drink.

(Mama places the glass in Christian's hand. She signals to the musicians to play.)

Raise your glass to him, and smile.
CHRISTIAN: Thank you, but I don't drink.

MAMA (*Whispered*): Oh, you most certainly do, today. You will drink every last drop of what he offers, and when he buys you another round you'll drink that as well. You will drink until he decides you've had enough.

(*Christian looks over at the smiling Osembenga. He raises his glass to Osembenga across the room, contemplating the drink for a long hard moment.*)

OSEMBENGA: Drink up!

CHRISTIAN: I—

MAMA: Please. (*Whispered*) He's a very important man.

CHRISTIAN: Please, Mama.

MAMA: He can help us, or he can cause us many problems. It's your decision. Remember, if you don't step on the dog's tail, he won't bite you.

OSEMBENGA: Drink up!

(*The Government Soldiers egg Christian on. Unnerved, Christian, slowly and with difficulty, drinks the liquor, wincing. Osembenga laughs. He signals for Mama to pour Christian another. She does. Again, the Soldiers cheer Christian on.*)

Good. (*Shouts*) To health and prosperity!

(*Christian contemplates the second drink. Osembenga raises his glass. Christian nervously knocks back the second shot of whiskey, and, again, winces. Osembenga smiles. He signals for Mama to pour another. The Soldiers cheer. Mama pours him another.*)

CHRISTIAN: Don't make—

MAMA: Trust me.

(*She places the glass in his hand. Christian walks over to Osembenga's table. We aren't sure whether he is going to*

throw the drink in his face or toast him. He forcefully thrusts
his drink in the air. Blackout.)

Scene 5

Morning. The bar. Sophie reads from the pages of a romance novel.
Josephine and Salima sit listening, rapt. It is a refuge.

SOPHIE *(Reading)*: "The others had left the party, they were
    alone. She was now painfully aware that there was only
    the kiss left between them. She felt herself stiffen as he
    leaned into her. The hairs on her forearms stood on end,
    and the room suddenly grew several degrees warmer—"
JOSEPHINE: Oh, kiss her!
SALIMA: Shh!
SOPHIE: "His lips met hers. She could taste him, smell him, and
    all at once her body was infused with—"

(Mama enters with the lockbox. Sophie protectively slips the
book behind her back. Mama grabs it.)

MAMA: What's this?
SOPHIE: . . . A romance, Uncle Christian bought it.
MAMA: A romance?
SOPHIE: Yes.

(Mama examines the book. The women's eyes plead with her
not to take it.)

MAMA: Josephine, we need water in the back, and Salima, the
    broom is waiting for you in the yard.
SALIMA: Ah, Mama, let her finish the chapter.
MAMA: Are you giving me lip? I didn't think so. Come here.
    Hurry.

(Salima reluctantly walks over to Mama. Mama grabs her wrist and runs her hand over Salima's stomach.)

You must be happy here. You're getting fat fat!
SALIMA: I didn't notice.
MAMA: Well, I have.

(Salima, petrified, isn't sure where Mama's going. Then:)

You did good last night.
SALIMA *(Surprised)*: Thank you.

(Mama tosses the book back to Sophie.)

JOSEPHINE: You don't care for romance, Mama?
MAMA: Me? No, the problem is I already know how it's going to end. There'll be kissing, fucking, a betrayal, and then the woman will foolishly surrender her heart to an undeserving man. Okay. Move. Move. Ach. Ach. Sophie wait.

(Salima grabs the broom and exits.)

JOSEPHINE *(Gesturing to Sophie)*: What about her?
MAMA: I need her help.
JOSEPHINE: Tst!
MAMA: You have a problem with that? You count good?

(Josephine stares down Sophie. Sophie isn't having it. Mama laughs. Salima pokes her head in the door.)

SALIMA: Mama. Someone's coming around the bend.
MAMA *(Surprised)*: So early?
JOSEPHINE: Tst! Another stupid miner looking to get his cock wet.
SALIMA: No, I think it's Mr. Harari.
JOSEPHINE: What?

SALIMA: "Come with me to the city, my darling."
JOSEPHINE: Don't hate!
SOPHIE: "I'm going to buy you a palace in Lebanon, my darling."

(This strikes a nerve.)

JOSEPHINE: Hey, hey. At least I have somebody, I take care of him good. And he comes back.

(Josephine seductively approaches Sophie. She grabs her close.)

Joke, laugh, *jolie fille*, but we all know a man wants a woman who's complete.
SOPHIE: Okay, stop—
JOSEPHINE: He wants her to open up and allow him to release himself, he wants to pour the whole world into her.
SOPHIE: I said stop!
JOSEPHINE: Can you be that woman?
MAMA: Let her alone. Go get the water!
JOSEPHINE: I was firstborn child! My father was chief!
MAMA: Yeah, and my father was whoever put money in my mama's pocket! Chief, farmer who the hell cares? Go!

(Josephine storms off. Salima follows.)

Give Josephine a good smack in the mouth, and she won't bother you no more.

(She plops the lockbox on the table.)

Here. Count last night's money. Let me know how we did.

(Sophie opens the lockbox. Mama skillfully funnels water into a whiskey bottle.)

I don't know where all these men are coming from, but I'm happy for it.

(Sophie pulls out the money, a worn ribbon, and then a small stone.)

SOPHIE: Why do you keep this pebble?

MAMA: That? It doesn't look like anything. Stupid man, give it to me to hold for one night of company and four beers not even cold enough to quench his thirst. He said he'd be back for it and he'd pay me. It's a raw diamond. It probably took him a half year of sifting through mud to dig it up, and he promised his simple wife a Chinese motor scooter and fabric from Senegal. And there it is, some unfortunate woman's dream.

SOPHIE: What will you do with it?

MAMA *(Chuckling to herself)*: Do? Ha!

(Mama knocks back a shot of watered-down whiskey.)

It still tastes like whiskey. I don't know, but as long as they are foolish enough to give it to me, I'll keep accepting it. My mother taught me that you can follow behind everyone and walk in the dust, or you can walk ahead through the unbroken thorny brush. You may get blood on your ankles, but you arrive first and not covered in the residue of others. This land is fertile and blessed in many regards, and the men ain't the only one's entitled to its bounty.

SOPHIE: What if the man comes back for his stone?

MAMA: A lot of people would sell it, run away. But it is my insurance policy, it is what keeps me from becoming like them. There must always be a part of you that this war can't touch. It's a damn shame, but I keep it for that stupid woman. Enough talk, how'd we do?

SOPHIE: Good. If we—

MAMA: We?

SOPHIE: Charged a little more for the beer, just a few more francs. By the end of the year we'll have enough to buy a new generator.

MAMA: Yeah? A new generator? Good. You're quick with num-
bers. Yes. You counted everything from last night. Your tips?
SOPHIE: Yes.
MAMA: Yes?

*(A moment. Mama reaches into Sophie's chest and produces
a fold of money.)*

MAMA: Is this yours?
SOPHIE: Yes. I was—
MAMA: Yes? So tell me what you're planning to do with my
money. *(With edge)* Cuz it's my money.
SOPHIE: I—
MAMA: I,I,I . . . what?
SOPHIE: It's not what you think, Mama.
MAMA: No, you're not trying to run off with my money? "Take
her in, give her food." Your uncle begged me. What am
I supposed to do? I trust you. Everyone say, she bad luck,
but I think this is a smart girl, maybe Mama won't have
to do everything by herself. You read books, you speak
good, like white man—but is this who you want to be?
SOPHIE: I'm sorry, Mama.
MAMA: No. No. I will put you out on your ass. I will let you walk
naked down that road, is that what you want? What did
you think you were going to do with my money?!

(Mama grabs Sophie, pulls her to the door.)

SOPHIE: Mama! Please! . . .
MAMA: You want to be out there? Huh? Huh? Then go! Go!

(Sophie struggles, terrified.)

Huh? What were you going to do?
SOPHIE: A man that come in here said he can help me. He said
there is an operation for girls.

MAMA: Don't you lie to me.

SOPHIE: Listen, listen, please listen, they can repair the damage.

(A moment. Mama releases Sophie.)

MAMA: An operation?

SOPHIE: Yes, he give me this paper. Look, look.

MAMA: And it can make it better?

SOPHIE: Yes.

(Mama makes a show of putting the money into her lockbox.)

MAMA: Hm. Congratulations! You're the first girl bold enough to steal from me. *(Laughs)* Where are your books?

SOPHIE: Under my bed.

MAMA: Go bring them to me. I know you better than you think, girl.

(The lights fade.)

Scene 6

The bar. Morning light pours in. Josephine struggles with a drunk Miner. She finally manages to push him out of the bar, then exits into the back. Salima quickly sneaks food from under the counter. She stuffs fufu into her mouth. The bird squawks as if to tell on her.

SALIMA: Shh! Shh!

(Christian, winded and on edge, comes rushing into the bar. He is covered in dirt.)

Professor!

CHRISTIAN: Get Mama!

(Salima quickly exits. Christian paces. Mama enters.)

MAMA: Professor! *(Beat)* What, what is it?
CHRISTIAN: The white pastor's dead.
MAMA: What?

(Christian sits, then immediately stands.)

CHRISTIAN: He was dead for over a week before anyone found his body. He was only a hundred meters from the chapel. The cook said it was Osembenga's soldiers. They accused the pastor of aiding rebels. Do you hear what I am saying?

(Mama takes in his words, they bite her.)

They cut him up beyond recognition. Cut out his eyes and tongue. *(Nauseated by the notion)*
MAMA: The pastor? I'm sorry to hear that.

(Mama pours herself a whiskey.)

CHRISTIAN: Can I have one of those, please?
MAMA: Are you sure?
CHRISTIAN: Just give it to me damn it!

(Mama hesitantly pours Christian a drink. She stares at him.)

What?

(He gulps it down.)

The policeman said there were no witnesses. No one saw anything, and so there is nothing he can do. Bury him, he said. Me? I barely know the man, and people who worked with him for years were mute, no one knew anything. He was butchered, and no one knows anything.

MAMA: Take it easy.

CHRISTIAN: These ignorant country boys, who wouldn't be able to tell left from right, they put on a uniform and suddenly they're making decisions for us. Give me another.

MAMA: The Fantas are cold.

CHRISTIAN: I don't want a Fanta.

(Mama reluctantly pours Christian another drink. His hand slightly quivers as he knocks back the liquor.)

They've killed a white man. Do you know what that means? A missionary. They're pushing this way. They won't think twice about killing us.

MAMA: A dead pastor, is just another dead man, and people here see that every day. I can't think about it right now. I have ten girls to feed, and a business to run.

(Mama buries her face in her palms, overwhelmed.)

CHRISTIAN: Come with me, Mama. We'll go to Kinshasa where there's no trouble. Between the two of us . . . The two of us. We'll open a small place. Serve food, drink, dancing.

(Mama isn't convinced. Christian reaches for the bottle of whiskey, she snatches it away. Christian slams the bar.

Two ragged Soldiers, Fortune and Simon, enter like a whirlwind. They carry beat-up rifles and wear dirty ill-fitting uniforms. Fortune also carries an iron pot. They are on edge, which makes Mama very uneasy.)

MAMA: Yes?

FORTUNE: Is this the place of Mama Nadi?

MAMA: Yes, that is me. What can I do for you?

FORTUNE: We'll have a meal and a beer.

MAMA: Okay, no problem. I have fish and fufu from last night.

FORTUNE: Yeah. Good. Good.

MAMA: It ain't hot.

SIMON: We'll have it.

(*Mama eyes the men suspiciously. Christian, petrified, does his best to mask it.*)

MAMA: Please don't be offended, but I'll need to see your money.

(*Fortune removes a pile of worn bills from his pocket. The men move to sit.*)

Hey. Hey. Hey. Empty your weapons.

(*The men hesitate.*)

SIMON: No, our wea—

MAMA: It's the rule. If you want to be fed.

(*The men reluctantly remove their clips from their guns and hand them to Mama.*)

FORTUNE (*To Christian*): Good morning.

CHRISTIAN: Good morning.

SIMON: Do you have a place for us to wash up?

FORTUNE: In the back maybe.

(*Fortune gestures toward the backdoor.*)

MAMA (*Suspicious*): I can bring you a basin of water.

(*They sit. Sophie enters, she's surprised to find Christian and the Soldiers.*)

SOPHIE: Uncle.

CHRISTIAN: *Bonjour, mon amour.*

SOPHIE: What happened to—

CHRISTIAN: Shh. I'm okay.

(*Sophie notes the caution in his tone.*)

FORTUNE AND SIMON: Good morning. How are you?

(*The men politely rise.*)

SOPHIE (*Timidly*): Good morning.

(*The men sit.*)

MAMA: Bring some water for the basin.
FORTUNE: Please.

(*Sophie exits with the basin. Mama serves beer.*)

Thank you.
MAMA: You come from the east?
FORTUNE: No.
MAMA: Farmers?
FORTUNE: NO! We're soldiers! We follow Commander Osembenga!

(*Sophie returns with the full basin, but Christian signals for her to leave. Christian grows increasingly nervous. He watches the men like a hawk.*)

MAMA: Easy. I don't mean to insult you, Soldier. But you look like good men. Men who don't follow trouble.

(*Fortune seems reluctant to speak.*)

SIMON: We are—
FORTUNE: I'm told there is a woman here named Salima. Is that true?

CHRISTIAN: There—

MAMA: Why? Who is looking for her?

FORTUNE: Is she here!? I asked you, is she here!?

MAMA: I'd adjust your tone, mister.

FORTUNE: Please, I'm looking for a woman named Salima.

MAMA: I have to ask inside.

(Christian and Mama exchange a look.)

FORTUNE: She's from Kaligili. She has a small scar on her right cheek. Just so.

MAMA: A lot of women come and go. I'll ask around. And may I say who's looking for her?

FORTUNE: Fortune, her husband.

(Christian registers this discovery.)

MAMA: Excuse me. I'll go ask inside.

(Mama exits. Christian disappears into his drink.)

SIMON: We'll find her, Fortune. C'mon, drink up. When was your last cold beer?

FORTUNE: I'm not thirsty.

(Simon drinks.)

SIMON: Ah, that's nice. It's nice, man.

(Fortune paces.)

FORTUNE: Come on, come on, where is she?

SIMON: Be patient. Man, if she's here we'll find her.

FORTUNE: Why is it taking so long?

SIMON: Take it easy.

FORTUNE: You heard it, the man on the road described Salima. It is her.

(Simon laughs.)

What?

(Fortune paces.)

SIMON: You say that every time. Maybe it is, maybe it isn't. We've been walking for months, and in every village there is a Salima. You are certain. So please, don't—

MAMA *(Reemerging)*: There is no Salima here.

FORTUNE *(Shocked)*: What? No! She is here!

MAMA: I'm sorry, you are mistaken. You got bad information.

FORTUNE: Salima! Salima Mukengeshayi!!

MAMA: I said she is not here.

FORTUNE: You lying witch! Salima!

MAMA: Call me names, but there's still no Salima here. I think maybe the woman you're looking for is dead.

FORTUNE: She is here! Goddamn you, she is here.

(Fortune flips over the table. Mama grabs a machete. Christian brandishes the whiskey bottle like a weapon.)

MAMA: Please, I said she is not here. And if you insist I will show you how serious I am.

SIMON: We don't want trouble.

MAMA: Now go. Get out! Get the hell out of here.

FORTUNE *(Shouts)*: Tell Salima, I will be back for her!

(The parrot raises hell. Christian scolds Mama with his eyes. Blackout.)

ACT TWO

Scene 1

Fortune, in his ill-fitting uniform, stands outside the bar, like a centurion guarding the gates.

Josephine teases two drunk Government Soldiers and a Miner. Guitar. Drums. Mama and Sophie sing a dance song. Mr. Harari and Christian watch. Festive.

MAMA *(Sings)*:

> Hey, monsieur, come play, monsieur,
> Hey, monsieur, come play, monsieur,
> The Congo sky rages electric
> As bullets fly like hell's rain,
> Wild flowers wilt and the forest decays.
> But here we're pouring Champagne.

MAMA AND SOPHIE *(Sing)*:

> Cuz a warrior knows no peace,
> When a hungry lion's awake.

But when that lion's asleep,
The warrior is free to play.

SOPHIE (Sings):

Drape your weariness on my shoulder,
Sweep travel dust from your heart.
Villages die as soldiers grow bolder,
We party as the world falls apart.

MAMA AND SOPHIE (Sing):

Cuz a warrior knows no peace,
When a hungry lion's awake.
But when that lion's asleep,
The warrior is free to play.

(The drum beats out a furious rhythm. Josephine answers
with a dance, which begins playfully, seductively, then slowly
becomes increasingly frenzied. She releases her anger, her
pain ... everything. She desperately grabs at the air as if trying to hold on to something. She abruptly stops, overwhelmed. Sophie goes to her aid.)

MAMA AND SOPHIE (Sing):

Hey, monsieur, come play, monsieur,
Hey, monsieur, come play, monsieur,

(Sophie leads a spent Josephine to the back.)

MAMA:

The door never closes at Mama's place.
The door never closes at Mama's place.

(Mr. Harari nurses a beer as he watches Sophie and Mama
sing. Christian, drunk and disheveled, struggles to remain
erect.)

MAMA (*Sings*):
> The door never closes at Mama's place.

(*Soldier laughter. Distant gunfire.*)

Scene 2

Lights fade. The back room.
Josephine sleeps. Salima quickly pulls down her shirt hiding her pregnant stomach as Mama enters eating a mango.

MAMA (*To Salima*): Are you going to hang here in the shadows until forever? I have thirsty miners with a good day in their pockets.

SALIMA: Sorry, Mama, but—

MAMA: I need one of you to go make them happy, show them their hard work isn't for naught. (*Clicks her tongue*) C'mon. C'mon.

SALIMA (*Whispered*): But . . .

MAMA: Josephine!

JOSEPHINE: Ah! Why is it always me?

(*Josephine rises. She exits in a huff, brushing past Sophie, who is just entering after bathing. Salima nervously looks to the door.*)

SALIMA: Is Fortune still outside?

MAMA: Your husband? Yes. He's still standing there, he couldn't be more quiet than if he were a stake driven into the ground. I don't like quiet men.

SALIMA: He's always been so.

MAMA: Well, I wish he wouldn't be "so" outside of my door.

(*Salima involuntarily smiles.*)

SALIMA: Why won't he go already? I don't want him to see me.

SOPHIE: He's not leaving until he sees you, Salima.

(Sophie dresses.)

MAMA: Ha. What for? So he can turn his lip up at her again.

SOPHIE: No. C'mon, he's been out there for two nights. If he doesn't love you, why would he still be there.

SALIMA: Yeah?

MAMA: Tst! Both of you are so stupid. He'll see you, love will flood into his eyes, he'll tell you everything you want to hear, and then one morning, I know how it happens, he will begin to ask ugly questions, but he won't be able to hear the answers. And no matter what you say, he won't be satisfied. I know. And, chérie, don't look away from me, will you be able to tell him the truth? Huh? We know, don't we? The woman he loved is dead.

SOPHIE: That's not true. He—

MAMA *(To Salima)*: He left her for dead. See. This is your home now. Mama takes care of you.

(Mama takes Salima in her arms.)

But if you want to go back out there, go. But they, your village, your people, they won't understand. Oh, they'll say they will, but they won't. Because, you know, underneath everything, they will be thinking she's damaged. She's been had by too many men. She let them, those dirty men, touch her. She's a whore. And Salima, are you strong enough to stomach their hate? It will be worse than anything you've felt yet.

SOPHIE: But he—

MAMA: I'm not being cruel, but your simple life, the one you remember, that . . . Yeah the one you're so fond of . . . it's vapor, chérie. It's gone.

(Tears flood Salima's eyes.)

Now, uh-uh, don't cry. We keep our faces pretty. I will
send him away. Okay? Okay?

SALIMA: Okay.

MAMA: We'll make him go away. Yeah?

SALIMA: Okay. Good.

SOPHIE: No, Mama, please, let her at least talk to him. He wants
to take her home.

MAMA: You read too many of those romance novels where
everything is forgiven with a kiss. Enough, my miners are
waiting.

(Mama suspiciously eyes Salima's belly and exits.)

SOPHIE: If you don't want to see him, then at least go out there
and tell him. He's been sitting outside in the rain for two
days, and he's not going to leave.

SALIMA: Let him sit.

SOPHIE: Go, talk to him. Maybe you'll feel differently.

SALIMA: He doesn't know that I'm pregnant. When he sees me,
he'll hate me all over again.

SOPHIE: You don't know that. He came all this way.

(A moment.)

SALIMA: Stupid man. Why did he have to come?

SOPHIE: All you ever talk about is wanting to get away from
here. Go with him, Salima. Get the hell out of here! Go!

SALIMA: He called me a filthy dog, and said I tempted them. Why
else would it happen? Five months in the bush, passed
between the soldiers like a wash rag. Used. I was made poi-
son by their fingers, that is what he said. He had no choice
but to turn away from me, because I dishonored him.

SOPHIE: He was hurting. It was sour pride.

SALIMA: Why are you defending him!? Then you go with him!

SOPHIE: I'm not def—

SALIMA: Do you know what I was doing on that morning? (*A calm washes over her*) I was working in our garden, picking the last of the sweet tomatoes. I put Beatrice down in the shade of a frangipani tree, because my back was giving me some trouble. Forgiven? Where was Fortune? He was in town fetching a new iron pot. "Go," I said. "Go, today, man, or you won't have dinner tonight!" I had been after him for a new pot for a month. And finally on that day the damn man had to go and get it. A new pot. The sun was about to crest, but I had to put in another hour before it got too hot. It was such a clear and open sky. This splendid bird, a peacock, had come into the garden to taunt me, and was showing off its feathers. I stooped down and called to the bird: "Wssht, Wssht." And I felt a shadow cut across my back, and when I stood four men were there over me, smiling, wicked schoolboy smiles. "Yes?" I said. And the tall soldier slammed the butt of his gun into my cheek. Just like that. It was so quick, I didn't even know I'd fallen to the ground. Where did they come from? How could I not have heard them?

SOPHIE: You don't have to—

SALIMA: One of the soldiers held me down with his foot. He was so heavy, thick like an ox and his boot was cracked and weathered like it had been left out in the rain for weeks. His boot was pressing my chest and the cracks in the leather had the look of drying sorghum. His foot was so heavy, and it was all I could see as the others . . . "took" me. My baby was crying. She was a good baby. Beatrice never cried, but she was crying, screaming. "Shhh," I said. "Shhh." And right then . . . (*Closes her eyes*) A soldier stomped on her head with his boot. And she was quiet.

(*A moment. Salima releases:*)

Where was everybody? WHERE WAS EVERYBODY?!

(Sophie hugs Salima.)

SOPHIE: It's okay. Take a breath.

SALIMA: I fought them!

SOPHIE: I know.

SALIMA: I did!

SOPHIE: I know.

SALIMA: But they still took me from my home. They took me through the bush—raiding thieves. Fucking demons! "She is for everyone, soup to be had before dinner," that is what someone said. They tied me to a tree by my foot, and the men came whenever they wanted soup. I make fires, I cook food, I listen to their stupid songs, I carry bullets, I clean wounds, I wash blood from their clothing, and, and, and . . . I lay there as they tore me to pieces, until I was raw . . . five months. Five months. Chained like a goat. These men fighting . . . fighting for our liberation. Still I close my eyes and I see such terrible things. Things I cannot stand to have in my head. How can men be this way?

(A moment.)

It was such a clear and open sky. So, so beautiful. How could I not hear them coming?

SOPHIE: Those men were on a path and we were there. It happened.

SALIMA: A peacock wandered into my garden, and the tomatoes were ripe beyond belief. Our fields of red sorghum were so perfect, it was going to be a fine season. Fortune thought so, too, and we could finally think about planning a trip on the ferry to visit his brother. Oh God please give me back that morning. "Forget the pot, Fortune. Stay . . ." "Stay," that's what I would tell him. What did I do, Sophie? I must have done something. How did I get in the middle of their fight?

SOPHIE: You were picking sweet tomatoes. That's all. You didn't do anything wrong.

(Sophie kisses Salima on the cheek.)

SALIMA: It isn't his baby. It's the child of a monster, and there's no telling what it will be. Now, he's willing to forgive me, and is it that simple, Sophie? But what happens when the baby is born, will he be able to forgive the child, will I? And, and . . . and even if I do, I don't think I'll be able to forgive him.

SOPHIE: You can't know that until you speak to him.

SALIMA: I walked into the family compound expecting wide open arms. An embrace. Five months, suffering. I suffered every single second of it. And my family gave me the back of their heads. And he, the man I loved since I was four-teen, chased me away with a green switch. He beat my ankles raw. And I dishonored him? I dishonored him?! Where was he? Buying a pot? He was too proud to bear my shame . . . but not proud enough to protect me from it. Let him sit in the rain.

SOPHIE: Is that really what you want?

SALIMA: Yes.

SOPHIE: He isn't going to leave.

SALIMA: Then I'm sorry for him.

(The lights shift to moonlight.)

Scene 3

Rain, moonlight. Outside the bar, Fortune stands in the rain. His posture is erect. Music and laughter pour out of the bar. Mama seductively stands in the doorway. She watches Fortune for a moment.

MAMA: The sky doesn't look like it's gonna let up for a long time. My mama used to say, "Careful of the cold rain, it carries more men to their death than a storm of arrows."

FORTUNE: Why won't you let me see her?

MAMA: Young man, the woman you're looking for isn't here. But if you want company, I have plenty of that. What do you like? *(Seductively)* I know the challenges of a soldier's life, I hear stories from men every day. And there's nothing better than a gentle hand to pluck out the thorns, and heal the heart.

(Mama runs her hand up her thigh. She laughs. Fortune turns away, disgusted. Mama smiles.)

FORTUNE: Please . . . tell my wife, I love her.

MAMA: Yeah. Yeah. I've heard it before. You're not the first man to come here for his wife. But, Soldier, are you sure this is the place you want to be looking for her?

FORTUNE: Here. Give this to her.

(Fortune lifts an iron pot.)

MAMA: A pot?

(Mama laughs.)

FORTUNE: Yes, please. Just give it to her.

MAMA: Very charming. A pot. Is this how you intend to woo a woman?

(Fortune shoves it into her hands.)

You're a nice-looking young man. You seem decent. Go from here. Take care of your land and your mother.

(Two tipsy Government Soldiers tumble out of the bar.)

GOVERNMENT SOLDIER #2: Just one more time. One. More. Time.
GOVERNMENT SOLDIER #3: Shut up! That girl doesn't want you.
GOVERNMENT SOLDIER #2: Oh yes, she do. She don't know it, but she do.

(Drunk, Government Soldier #2 crumples to the ground. Government Soldier #3 finds this hysterically funny.)

MAMA *(To Fortune)*: Go home. Have I made myself clear?

(Mama goes into the bar. Fortune fumes.)

FORTUNE *(To Soldier #3)*: Idiot! Pick him up! God is watching you.

(Soldier #3 lifts up his friend, as Simon, out of breath, comes running up to Fortune. Josephine seductively fills the doorway.)

JOSEPHINE: Ay! Ay! Don't leave me so soon. Where are you going?
SIMON: Fortune! Fortune!

(The two Soldiers disappear into the night.)

JOSEPHINE: Come back! Let me show you something sweet and pretty. Come.

(Josephine laughs.)

SIMON: Fortune! *(He doubles-over out of breath)* The commander is gathering everyone. We march out tomorrow morning. The militia is moving on the next village.
FORTUNE: What about Salima? I can't leave her.
SIMON: But we have our orders. We have to go.
JOSEPHINE *(Seductively)*: Hello, baby. Come say hello to me.
SIMON *(His face lights up)*: God help me, look at that sweetness.

(Simon licks his lips. Josephine does several down-and-dirty pelvic thrusts. Fortune tries not to smile.)

Quick. Let me hold some money, so I can go inside and talk to this good-time girl. C'mon, c'mon . . . c'mon, Fortune. *(To Josephine)* What's your name?

JOSEPHINE: Josephine. Come inside, baby.

FORTUNE: Don't let the witch tempt you.

(Josephine laughs and disappears inside.)

SIMON: Let's enjoy ourselves, man, tonight . . . At least let me have one more taste of pleasure. A little taste. Just the tip of my tongue. C'mon, man, let me hold some money. *(Laughs)*

(Fortune does not respond. He silently prays.)

How long are you gonna do this? Huh? We've been up and down the road. It's time to consider that maybe she's dead.

FORTUNE: Then leave!

(Simon, frustrated, starts to go.)

SIMON: This makes no sense. You can't stay here, the rebel militia are moving this way. And if they find you, they'll kill you. We have to go by morning, with or without her.

FORTUNE: Go!

SIMON: Are you sure? You're becoming like Emmanuel Bwiza whose wife drowned in the river when we were children. Remember, the old fool got drunk on bitterness and lost heself. Look here, Fortune, the men are making a joke of you. They're saying, "Why won't the man just take another woman." "Why is he chasing a damaged girl?"

(Fortune, enraged, grabs Simon around the neck. The friends struggle.)

FORTUNE *(Challenges)*: Say it again!
SIMON: It is not me saying it. It is the other men in the brigade.
FORTUNE: Who?
SIMON: If I tell you, are you going to fight all of them?
FORTUNE: Tell me who!
SIMON: Everyone. Every damn one of them. Okay.

(Fortune releases Simon.)

Man, *mavi yako!* It's time to forget her. I'm your cousin, and for three months I've been walking with you, right? Got dirty, got bloody with you. But now, I'm begging you, stop looking. It's time.
FORTUNE: No, I've prayed on this.
SIMON: Come out of the rain. We'll go inside and spend the last of our money, and forget her. C'mon, Fortune. Let's get stupid drunk. Huh? Huh? C'mon.

(Simon tries to drag Fortune into the bar. Fortune resists. Fuming, he raises his fist to Simon.)

If you are angry, then be angry at the men who took her. Think about how they did you, they reached right into your pocket and stole from you. I know Salima since we were children. I love her the same as you. She'd want you to avenge her honor. That is the only way to heal your soul.

(Fortune contemplates his words.)

FORTUNE: Kill?
SIMON: Yes.

(Fortune laughs ironically.)

FORTUNE: We are farmers. What are we doing? They tell us shoot and we shoot. But for what are we getting? Salima? A better crop? No, man, we're moving further and further away from home. I want my wife! That's all. I want my family.

SIMON: The commander gave us orders to kill all deserters.

FORTUNE: Are you going to kill me?

(A moment.)

SIMON: I wouldn't have said it a month ago, but I'll say it now. She's gone.

(Simon walks off into the darkness. Fortune stands outside the bar in the pouring rain.
Gunfire. A firefight. The sounds of the forest.)

Scene 4

The bar. Christian, drunk and haggard, is in the middle of an energetic story. He stands at the bar nursing a beer. Mr. Harari, Sophie and Mama stand around listening.

CHRISTIAN *(With urgency)*: No, no, no . . . listen, listen to me, I've just come from there, and it's true. I saw a boy, take a machete to a man, sever his neck, a clean blow, and lift the head in the air like a trophy. May God be my witness. Men were hollering: "We strong warriors, we taste victory. We will kill!"

MAMA: Shh, keep it down?!

CHRISTIAN: Oh shit, my hand, my hand is still shaking. This . . . this man Osembenga is evil. He plays at democracy. This word we bandy about, "democracy," and the first opportunity we get, we spit on our neighbors and why? Because he has cattle and I don't. Because he is and I am not. But nobody has and nobody will have, except for men like you, Mr. Harari, who have the good sense to come and go, and not give a damn.

MAMA: Oh, hush up.

CHRISTIAN: But we have to pretend that all this ugliness means nothing. We wash the blood off with buckets of frigid water, and whitewash our walls. Our leaders tell us: "Follow my rules, your life will be better," their doctors say, "Take this pill, your life will be better," "Plant these seeds, your life will better," "Read this book, your life will be better," "Kill your neighbor, your life will be better—"

MAMA: Stop. Take it outside. You know I don't allow this talk in here. My doors are open to everybody. And that way trouble doesn't settle here.

CHRISTIAN: Well, someone has to say it, otherwise what? We let it go on. Huh?

MAMA: Professor, enough! Stop it now. Leave the philosophizing and preaching to the wretched politicians. I mean it! I won't have it here!

CHRISTIAN: One day it will be at your door, Mama.

MAMA: And then I'll shut it. People come here to leave behind what ever mess they've made out there. That includes you, professor.

(Two Rebel Soldiers, fresh from battle, appear from the back of the bar in various stages of undress. Josephine and Kisembe, doped-up and on edge, also enter from the back. Kisembe has scary unpredictable energy. Josephine buttons his shirt. He pushes her away.)

Sophie, turn on the music.

(Sophie turns on the radio. Congolese hip-hop music plays. Christian attempts to disappear behind his drink. Sophie

stands behind the bar, drying glasses, trying not to be noticed. Mama walks over to greet the men. The Parrot squawks.)

Colonel Kisembe, I hope my girls gave you good company.

KISEMBE: Very. It is good to be back, Mama. Where's everyone?

MAMA: You tell me. It's been this way for a week. I haven't seen but a handful of miners. I bake bread and it goes stale.

KISEMBE: It is Commander Osembenga. He is giving us some trouble.

CHRISTIAN: He's a crazy bastard!

KISEMBE: His men set fire to several of our villages, now everyone has fled deeper into the bush.

MAMA: I saw smoke over the trees.

REBEL SOLDIER #3: The mission. They burn everything to save bullets.

(Sophie gasps and covers her mouth.)

KISEMBE: They took machetes to anything that moves. This is their justice.

(Josephine spots Mr. Harari. She is torn about where to place her affection.)

Believe me, when we find Osembenga and his collaborators, he will be shown the same mercy he showed our people. It's what they deserve. *(To Christian)* Am I right? You? Am I right?

CHRISTIAN *(Reluctantly)*: You are right. But—

KISEMBE: I'm sorry. It's how it has to be. They have done this to us. I see you agree, Mama.

MAMA: Of course.

(Everyone in the bar grows uneasy, afraid of Kisembe's intense erratic energy. They're barely listening to his rhetoric, instead focused on trying not to set him off.)

KISEMBE: They say we are the renegades. We don't respect the rule of law . . . but how else do we protect ourselves against their aggression? Huh? How do we feed our families? Ay? They bring soldiers from Uganda, drive us from our land and make us refugees . . . and then turn us into criminals when we protest or try to protect ourselves. How can we let the government carve up our most valuable land to serve to companies in China. It's our land. Ask the Mbuti, they can describe every inch of the forest as if were their own flesh. Am I telling the truth?

MAMA: Here's to the truth!

(Kisembe, pleased with his own words, places a cigarette in his mouth. A young Rebel Soldier quickly lights it for him. Kisembe challenges Christian with his eyes. Christian averts his gaze. He nervously raises his glass.)

CHRISTIAN: The truth!

(A moment. Mr. Harari uses the awkward silence to interject.)

MR. HARARI: Has, um, Osembenga shut down production at Yaka-yaka mine?

KISEMBE: And you are?

MR. HARARI: I'm sorry, Colonel, may I offer you my card?

(Mr. Harari passes Kisembe his card. Kisembe examines it.)

KISEMBE: Ha-ra-i?

MR. HARARI: Aziz Harari. Yes. Please. I handle mostly minerals, some precious stones, but I have contacts for everything. My mobile is always on. Let me buy you a drink.

(Mr. Harari signals Sophie to bring a bottle of whiskey over to Kisembe. She pours two glasses.)

KISEMBE: Thank you.

(Kisembe takes the bottle of whiskey and slips the card into his pocket, by way of dismissing Mr. Harari, who backs away. Mama wraps her arms around Kisembe's shoulders.)

MAMA: Come, gentlemen. You will be treated like warriors here.
KISEMBE: I wish we could stay all night, but duty calls.

(Kisembe signals to his men. They follow him toward the door.)

MAMA: No! So soon? Josephine!

(Mama signals to Josephine, who refuses to budge. Instead she sits on Mr. Harari's lap. Mr. Harari tenses.)

MR. HARARI (Whispers): Go!
JOSEPHINE: No.

(Kisembe and his men collect their guns and leave. A moment. A huge sigh of relief. Exhale. Christian slaps his thigh and stands. He does a spot-on impersonation of the haughty swagger of the rebel leader.)

CHRISTIAN: "Girl. Quick. Quick. Bring me a beer, so I can wash it down with Osembenga's blood."

(Sophie and Josephine laugh. Mr. Harari is too nervous to enjoy the show.)

SOPHIE: Yes, Colonel.
CHRISTIAN (Continuing to imitate Kisembe): "Woman, are you addressing me as 'Colonel'?"
SOPHIE: Yes, Colonel.

CHRISTIAN: "Don't you know who I am? I am from here on in to be known as the Great Commander of All Things Wise and Wonderful, with the Heart of a Hundred Lions in Battle."

SOPHIE: I'm so sorry, Great Commander of All Things Wise and . . .

CHRISTIAN: "Wonderful with the Heart of a Hundred Lions in Battle. Don't you forget that!"

(Christian does a playful mocking warrior dance. Josephine taps out a rhythm on the counter. A Drummer joins in. Mama laughs.)

MAMA: You are a fool!

(Mama retreats to the back with empty bottles. Unseen, the formidable Commander Osembenga and a sullen Government Soldier, Laurent, enter. They wear black berets and muddy uniforms. A moment. Christian stops his dance abruptly.)

OSEMBENGA: Don't stop you. Go on.

CHRISTIAN: Commander Osembenga.

OSEMBENGA: Continue.

(Osembenga smiles and claps his hands. Christian continues his dance, now drained of its verve and humor. Osembenga laughs. Then he stops clapping, releasing Christian from the dance. Christian, humiliated, retreats to the bar. Osembenga acknowledges Mr. Harari with a polite nod.)

Where is Mama?

SOPHIE: She's in the back. *(Yells)* Mama! Mama!

OSEMBENGA *(Suspiciously)*: I saw a truck leaving? Whose was it?

CHRISTIAN *(Lying)*: Uh . . . aid worker.

OSEMBENGA: Oh? Good-looking vehicle. Expensive. Eight cylinders.

CHRISTIAN: Yes.

OSEMBENGA: Sturdy. It looked like it could take the road during rainy season.

CHRISTIAN: Probably.

(Osembenga approves.)

SOPHIE: Mama!

MAMA *(Entering from off, annoyed)*: Why are you calling me?! You know I'm busy.

(Mama stops short when she sees Osembenga. She conjures a warm smile.)

(Surprised) Commander Osembenga. *Karibu.* *(Nervously)* We . . . how are you?

(Mama glances at the door.)

OSEMBENGA: Run ragged, if the truth be told. Two Primus, cold, and a pack of cigarettes.

(Mama directs Sophie to get the beer. Osembenga strokes Mama's backside. She playfully swats away his hand.)

You look good, today.

MAMA: You should have seen me yesterday.

OSEMBENGA: I wish I had, but I was otherwise engaged.

MAMA: Yeah? We heard you had some trouble. Kisembe.

OSEMBENGA: Is that what is being said? Not trouble! Slight irritation. But you'd be pleased to know, we're close to shutting down Kisembe and his militia. We finally have him on the run. He won't be troubling the people here very much longer.

MAMA: Is that so?

OSEMBENGA: My guess, he's heading east. He'll need to come through here. He can't hide from me. It's the only passable road.

MAMA: I saw smoke over the trees.

OSEMBENGA: That bastard and his cronies attacked the hospital.

MR. HARARI: The hospital? Why?

OSEMBENGA: Because they are imbeciles. I don't know. Looking for medicine. Speed. Morphine. Who the hell knows? They rounded-up and killed mostly Hema patients. *(To Sophie)* Tsst. Tsst. You, bring me some groundnuts. *(To Mama)* It was chaos. When we arrived we found the hospital staff tied by their hands and cut up like meat.

LAURENT: One man's heart was missing.

(Sophie covers her mouth with disgust.)

MAMA *(Disgusted)*: What?

OSEMBENGA: And he accuses us of being the barbarians? Don't worry, I've given my soldiers the liberty to control the situation. I am afraid this is what must be done. They force our hand.

(Osembenga takes sadistic delight in this notion. Sophie cringes as she places beer and peanuts on the table for the Soldiers. Osembenga grabs Sophie's wrist, and pulls her toward him.)

(Laughing) Come here, you pretty pretty thing. What? You don't like what I'm wearing?

(Sophie tries to gently pry herself loose. Christian, sensing tension, moves toward them. Laurent rises.)

You don't like men in uniforms? You don't like men, maybe. Is that it?

(A moment. Sophie now struggles to free herself.)

MAMA *(Sensing the tension)*: Sophie, come here. Let—
OSEMBENGA *(Smiling)*: Hey. We are talking. We are talking, yeah?

(Osembenga pulls Sophie onto his lap. He shoves his hand up her skirt. She gasps and struggles harder.)

Am I ugly? Is that what you're trying to tell me.
SOPHIE *(Hisses)*: Let go of me!

(Sophie violently pushes away from Osembenga. Christian rushes in to protect her, as Osembenga lunges for her. Mama blocks Osembenga's path. Laurent rises to aid Osembenga.)

MAMA: Sophie, shush! Enough. Commander, ignore her, there are other girls for you. Come. Come.
OSEMBENGA: Bring this girl around back, my men will teach her a lesson. She needs proper schooling.

(Laurent shoves Christian out of the way, and grabs Sophie. This is the first time we've seen Mama scared. Sophie spits on Osembenga's feet.)

MAMA: Sophie.

(Mama, horrified, bends down and wipes the spit from Osembenga's shoes. Osembenga glares at Sophie.)

SOPHIE *(Shouting as if possessed)*: I am dead.
MAMA: No!
SOPHIE *(Possessed)*: I am dead! Fuck a corpse! What would that make you?

(Osembenga is thrown.)

OSEMBENGA: I'm trying to bring order here, and this girl spits on my feet. Do you see what I have to deal with? Do you? This is the problem.

(Christian quickly pulls Sophie away.)

MAMA: Gentlemen, Commander, this is not our way . . . we want you to be comfortable and happy here, let me show you the pleasures of Mama Nadi's.

(A moment. A standoff.)

OSEMBENGA: Then, Mama, you show me.

(Osembenga checks his anger. He smiles. Mama understands. She follows Osembenga into the back. Sophie desperately scrubs her hands in the basin. Mr. Harari pours himself a healthy drink.)

MR. HARARI: Okay. Let's not overreact. Everything's going to be fine.

CHRISTIAN *(Whispers)*: Sophie, are you crazy? What are you doing?

(Josephine compassionately stops Sophie, who is scrubbing her hands raw.)

JOSEPHINE: Stop it. Stop it. *(Hugs Sophie tightly)* Shh. Shh.

(Mama furiously reenters. She slaps Sophie across the face.)

MAMA: Next time I will put you out for the vultures. I don't care if that was the man who slit your mother's throat. Do you understand me? You could have gotten all of us killed. What do you have to say to me?

SOPHIE: Sorry, Mama.

MAMA: You're lucky the commander is generous. I had to plead with him to give you another chance. Now you go in there, and you make sure that his cock is clean. Am I making myself clear?

SOPHIE: Please—

MAMA: Now get outta my sight.

(Mama grabs Sophie and thrusts her into the back. Mr. Harari, Christian and Josephine stare at Mama. A moment. Mama goes behind the bar and pours herself a drink.)

What?

CHRISTIAN: Don't make her do that! This girl is—

MAMA: What if Osembenga had been more than offended. What then? Who would protect my business if he turned on me? It is but for the grace of God, that he didn't beat her to the ground. And now I have to give away business to keep him and his filthy soldiers happy.

CHRISTIAN: But if—

MAMA: Not a word from you. You have a problem, then leave.

CHRISTIAN: "Business." When you say it, it sounds vulgar, polluted.

MAMA: Are you going to lecture me, professor? Turn your dirty finger away from me.

(Christian is stung by her words.)

CHRISTIAN: Mama?

MAMA: What, chérie? *(Laughs)*

CHRISTIAN *(Wounded)*: Forget it! Bring me another beer. There's my money. *(Slams the money down on the counter)* You understand *that*, don't you? You like that? There's your fucking money.

(Mama slowly picks up the money and puts it in her apron. She ceremoniously cracks open a beer and places it in front of Christian.)

MAMA: Drink up, you fucking drunk.

CHRISTIAN: What's wrong with you?

(Christian snatches up his beer. He drinks it down quickly and deliberately.)

MAMA: You men kill me. You come in here, drink your beer, take your pleasure, and then wanna judge the way I run my "business." The front door swings both ways. I don't force anyone's hand. My girls, Emilene, Mazima, Josephine, ask them, they'd rather be here, than back out there in their villages where they are taken without regard. They're safer with me than in their own homes, because this country is picked clean, while men, poets like you, drink beer, eat nuts and look for some place to disappear. And I am without mercy, is that what you're saying? Because I give them something other than a beggar's cup. *(With ferocity)* I didn't come here as Mama Nadi, I found her the same way miners find their wealth in the muck. I stumbled off of that road without two twigs to start a fire. I turned a basket of sweets and soggy biscuits into a business. I don't give a damn what any of you think. This is my place, Mama Nadi's.

(Christian crosses to leave.)

Of course.

(Mama's words stop him.)

CHRISTIAN:
>The black rope of water towing
>A rusted ferry fighting the current of time,
>An insatiable flow,
>Drifting

Without enough kerosene to get through the dark
   nights,
The destination always a port away.

MAMA *(Spits)*: It's wind. If you can't place it on a scale, it's
nothing.

(Christian heads for the door.)

You'll be back when you need another beer.
CHRISTIAN: I don't think so.

*(Christian absorbs the blow, then storms outside in a huff.
Josephine and Mr. Harari exit to the back. Mama is left alone
to contemplate her actions.)*

Scene 5

*Outside the bar. Osembenga and Laurent stumble out of Mama
Nadi's place, laughing.*

OSEMBENGA: I always like the taste of something new.
FORTUNE *(Approaching them)*: Commander! Commander!
OSEMBENGA: Yes?
FORTUNE: I'm sorry to disturb you, but I . . .
OSEMBENGA: Yes?
FORTUNE: I saw Jerome Kisembe.
OSEMBENGA: Who are you?
FORTUNE: I am Fortune Mukengeshayi, I'm with your brigade.
OSEMBENGA: Jerome Kisembe?
FORTUNE: Yes . . . He was inside Mama Nadi's.
OSEMBENGA: Inside here?
FORTUNE: Yes, I saw him. She was hiding him. I heard him say
the rebels are heading south along this road. He will join
them tomorrow.

OSEMBENGA: Mama Nadi's?! Here?!

FORTUNE: He drove south in a white truck! Please, she is holding my wife. I just want to get her back.

OSEMBENGA *(To Laurent)*: Quick, quick. We'll go after him. Call ahead, prepare the brigade to move out.

(They quickly exit.)

Scene 6

Dawn. Morning light pours into the bar. Mr. Harari paces. His traveling bag is perched near the door. Mama wipes down the bar.

MAMA: Would you like a drink while you wait?

(Artillery fire, closer than expected.)

MR. HARARI: Yes. Thank you. A little palm wine.

(Mama, settles her nerves, and pours them both a palm wine.)

MAMA: It looks like it's going to rain, you might wanna wait until—

MR. HARARI: I can't. Thank goodness, I found a lift with one of the aid workers. My driver, fucking idiot, took off last night. *(Jokes)* Apparently he doesn't care for the sound of gunfire.

MAMA: I told you, you didn't pay him enough.

MR. HARARI: This fucking war, ay mother, no one owns it! It's everybody's and nobody's.

MAMA: Tst!

MR. HARARI: It keeps fracturing and redefining itself. Militias form overnight, and suddenly a drunken foot solider with a tribal vendetta is a rebel leader, and in possession of half of the enriched land, but you can't reason with him, because he's only thinking as far as his next drink.

MAMA: Yes, and what is new?

MR. HARARI: The man I shake hands with in the morning is my enemy by sundown. And why? His whims. Because?! His witch doctor says I'm the enemy. I don't know whose hand to grease other than the one directly in front of me. At least I understood Mobutu's brand of chaos. Now, I'm a relative beginner, I must relearn the terms every few months, and make new friends, but who? It's difficult to say, so I must befriend everybody and nobody. And it's utterly exhausting.

MAMA: Let all the mother-hating soldiers fight it out. Cuz, in the end, do you think that will change anything here?

MR. HARARI: God only knows. The main road is crowded with folks heading east. There is no shame in leaving, Mama. Part of being in business is knowing when to cut your losses and get out.

MAMA: I have the only pool table in fifty kilometers. Where will people drink if anything happens to me?

MR. HARARI: The commander knows Kisembe was here. Eventually you must fly your colors. Take a side.

MAMA: He pays me in gold, he pays me in coltan. What is worth more? You tell me. What is their argument? I don't know. Who will win? Who cares? There's an old proverb, "Two hungry birds fight over a kernel, just then a third one swoops down and carries it off. Whoops!"

MR. HARARI: You are the most devilish of optimists. You—I don't worry so much about you. But what about a lovely girl like Sophie?

(His words hit her. Mr. Harari knocks back his drink, then heads for the door, looking out for his ride.)

Until next time!

(Distant gunfire. Mr. Harari anxiously stands in the doorway. Mama goes to the bar, she appears conflicted. An internal battle.)

MAMA: Ah . . . One thing, Mr. Harari. Before you leave, can I ask you a favor?

MR. HARARI: Of course.

(Mama opens the lockbox, and carefully lays out the diamond.)

MAMA: This.

(Mr. Harari's eyes light up.)

MR. HARARI: Your insurance policy.

MAMA *(With irony)*: Yes. My restaurant, my garden to dig in, and a chief's fortune of cows. *(Laughs)*

MR. HARARI: You are ready to sell?

MAMA: Yes. Take this. *(Hands him Sophie's piece of paper)* It has the name of a man in Bunia, a doctor. *(With urgency)* He won't trouble you with questions. Use my name.

MR. HARARI: Slow, slow, what do you want me—

MAMA: Just listen. I want you to take her to—

MR. HARARI *(Confused)*: Josephine? *(Genuinely surprised)* Be realistic, how would a girl like Josephine survive in the city.

MAMA: No, listen—

MR. HARARI: I can't. She is a country thing, not refined at all.

MAMA: No, listen . . . I'm talking about Sophie. This will raise enough money for an operation, and whatever she needs to get settled.

MR. HARARI: Sophie?

MAMA: Yes.

MR. HARARI: Why? Operation? What?

MAMA: It's a long conversation, and there isn't time.

MR. HARARI: This is more than—

MAMA: Enough for a life. I know.

MR. HARARI: Are you sure? This diamond will fetch a fairly decent price, you can settle over the border in Uganda. Start fresh.

MAMA: I have ten girls here. What will I do with them? Is there enough room for all of us in the car. No. I can't go. Since I was young, people have found reasons to push me out of my home, men have laid claim to my possessions, but I am not running now. This is my place. Mama Nadi's.

MR. HARARI: But I'm not—

MAMA: You do this for me. I don't want the other women to know. So let's do this quickly.

MR. HARARI: And the doctor's name is on the paper. I'm to call when I get there.

MAMA: Yes. And you give Sophie the money. The money for the stone. Understand. Promise me. It's important. All of it.

MR. HARARI: . . . Yes. Are you sure?

MAMA: Yes.

(Mama reluctantly passes the diamond to Mr. Harari.)

Thank you. I'll get her.

(Mama quickly exits. Mr. Harari examines the diamond. An Aid Worker comes rushing in.)

AID WORKER: I'm loaded. We have to go now! Now! Three vehicles are coming in fast. We can't be here.

MR. HARARI: But . . . What about—

AID WORKER *(Panicked)*: Now! I can't wait. C'mon. C'mon.

(Distant gunfire.)

MR. HARARI: I have to—

AID WORKER: They'll be okay. Us, men, they'll come after us—

MR. HARARI: One minute. *(Calling to Mama, off)* Mama! Mama! Come! Mama! I—

AID WORKER: I have to go! I can't wait.

(The Aid Worker doesn't have time to listen. He races out. The engine revs.)

MR. HARARI: Mama! Mama!

(Mr. Harari seems torn, a moment, then he decides. He places the diamond in his pocket and leaves. Silence. Then distant gunfire. Mama enters, frantically pulling Sophie.)

MAMA: When you get there, he has the money to take care of everything. Settle. Make a good life, hear.
SOPHIE: Why are you doing this for me?
MAMA: Stop, don't ask me stupid questions, just go. Go!

(She tucks a piece of paper into Sophie's hand.)

This is my cousin's wife, all I have is her address. But a motorbike will take you. You say that I am your friend.
SOPHIE: Thank you, Mama. I—
MAMA: No time. You send word through Mr. Harari. Let me know that everything goes well. Okay.

(Sophie hugs Mama. She exits. Mama, elated, goes to pour herself a celebratory drink. She doesn't see Sophie reenter until:)

SOPHIE: He's gone.

(The stage is flooded with intense light. The sound of chaos, shouting, gunfire, grows with intensity. Government Soldiers pour in. A siege. A white hot flash. The generator blows! Streams of natural light pour into the bar. Fortune, Commander Osembenga, Simon and Soldiers stand over Sophie and Mama.)

FORTUNE: He was here! I saw him here!

(Osembenga stands over Mama.)

OSEMBENGA: This soldier said he saw Jerome Kisembe here.

MAMA: This soldier is a liar.

FORTUNE: I swear to you! He was here with two men. The same night you were here, Commander!

MAMA: We are friends. Why would I lie to you? This soldier has been menacing us for days. He's crazy. A liar!

FORTUNE: This woman is the devil! She's a witch! She enchanted my wife.

OSEMBENGA: Again. Where is Kisembe?

MAMA: I don't know. Why would I play these games? Don't you think I know better. He is a simple digger. And me, I wouldn't give him what he wants, so he tells tales. Commander, we are friends. You know me. I am with you. Of course. Come, let me get you some whiskey—

OSEMBENGA: *Funga kinua yaké!*

(Osembenga signals to his Soldiers. Chaos. They find Mama's lockbox, break it open and take her money. A Soldier drags Josephine from the back. They throw Mama, Sophie and Josephine onto the floor.)

MAMA: NO!

OSEMBENGA: This can stop. Tell me where I can find Kisembe.

MAMA: I don't know where he is.

OSEMBENGA *(Points to Josephine)*: Take that one.

(A Soldier grabs Josephine. He is ready to sexually violate her. Josephine desperately struggles to get away. The Soldier tears away at her clothing. The women scream, fight.)

JOSEPHINE: No! No! Tell him, Mama. He was here.

(Osembenga turns his rage on Mama.)

MAMA: Please!

(Salima slowly enters as if in a trance. A pool of blood forms in the middle of her dress, blood drips down her legs.)

SALIMA *(Screams)*: STOP! Stop it!

FORTUNE: Salima!

SALIMA *(Screams)*: For the love of God, stop this! Haven't you done enough to us. Enough! Enough!

(The Soldiers stop abruptly, shocked by Salima's defiant voice.)

MAMA: What did you do?!

(Fortune violently pushes the Soldiers out of the way and races to Salima.)

FORTUNE: Salima! Salima!

SALIMA: Fortune.

(Fortune scoops Salima into his arms. Mama breaks away from the Soldiers.)

MAMA: Quick go get some hot water and cloth. Salima look at me. You have to look at me, keep your eyes on me. Don't think of anything else. C'mon look at me.

(Salima smiles triumphantly. She takes Fortune's hand.)

SALIMA *(To Osembenga, the Soldiers and Fortune)*: You will not fight your battles on my body anymore.

(Salima collapses to the floor. Fortune cradles her in his arms. She dies. Blackout.)

Scene 7

The sounds of the tropical Ituri rain forest. The bar. The bird quietly chatters. Sophie methodically sweeps the dirt floor with a thatched broom. Josephine washes the countertop. Mama stands in the doorway.

SOPHIE *(Sings):*

>Have another beer, my friend,
>Douse the fire of your fears, my friend,
>Get drunk and foolish on the moment,
>Brush aside the day's heavy judgment.

(Mama anxiously watches the road. Excited, she spots a passing truck.)

SOPHIE *(Sings):*

>Cuz you come here to forget,
>You say drive away all regret,
>And dance like it's the ending . . .

MAMA: Dust rising.

JOSEPHINE *(Eagerly):* Who is it?

MAMA *(Excited):* I don't know. Blue helmets heading north. Hello? Hello?

(Mama seductively waves. Nothing. Disappointed, she retreats to the table.)

Damn them. How the hell are we supposed to do business? They're draining our blood.

JOSEPHINE: Hey, Sophie, give me a hand.

(Josephine and Sophie pick up the basin of water and exit. Mama buries her face in her hands. Christian enters. He whistles. Mama looks up, doing her best to contain her excite-

ment. Christian brushes the travel dust from his brand-new brown suit.)

MAMA: Look who it is. The wind could have brought me a pay-ing customer, but instead I get you.

CHRISTIAN: Lovely. I'm glad to see after all these months you haven't lost any of your wonderful charm. You're looking fine as ever.

MAMA: Yeah? I'm making do with nothing.

(Christian smiles.)

Who'd you bribe to get past the roadblock?

CHRISTIAN: I have my ways, and as it turns out the officer on duty has a fondness for Nigerian soap operas and Belgian chocolates.

(Mama finally lets herself smile.)

I'm surprised to find you're still here.

MAMA: Were you expecting me to disappear into the forest and live off roots with the Mbuti? I'm staying put. The war's on the back of the gold diggers, you follow them you fol-low trouble. What are you wearing?

CHRISTIAN: You like?

MAMA: They didn't have your size?

CHRISTIAN: Very funny. Chérie, your eyes tell me everything I need to know.

MAMA: Tst!

CHRISTIAN: What you have something in your teeth?

MAMA: Business must be good. Yeah?

CHRISTIAN: No, but a man's got to have at least one smart change of clothing, even in times like these . . . I heard what happened.

(A moment.)

MAMA: *C'est la vie.* Salima was a good girl.

(Sophie enters.)

SOPHIE: Uncle!

(They exchange a long hug.)

CHRISTIAN: Sophie, *mon amour.* I have something for you.
SOPHIE: *Un livre?*
CHRISTIAN: . . . Yes.
SOPHIE: Merci.

*(He hands her a package. She rips open the brown paper. She
pulls out a handful of magazines and a book.)*

CHRISTIAN: And this. A letter from your mother. Don't expect
too much.

(Sophie, shocked, grabs the letter.)

SOPHIE *(Overwhelmed)*: Excuse me.
CHRISTIAN: Go!

(Sophie exits.)

MAMA: I'm surprised to see you. I thought you were through
with me.
CHRISTIAN: I was. I didn't come here to see you.
MAMA *(Wounded)*: Oh?
CHRISTIAN: And—
MAMA: Yes?

(A moment.)

. . . Hello, yes?

CHRISTIAN *(Hesitantly, but genuinely)*: I . . . I debated whether even to come, but damn it, I missed you.

(Mama laughs.)

You have nothing to say to me?
MAMA: Do you really want me to respond to your foolishness?
CHRISTIAN *(Wounded)*: You are a mean-spirited woman. I don't know why I expect the sun to shine where only mold thrives.

(His frankness catches Mama off guard.)

MAMA: I don't like your tone.
CHRISTIAN: We have unfinished "business"!
MAMA: Look around, there's no business here. There's nothing left.

(Christian looks around. He looks at Mama. He shakes his head and smiles.)

CHRISTIAN *(Blurts)*: Then, Mama, settle down with me.
MAMA: Go home!
CHRISTIAN: What?!
MAMA: You heard me, go the hell home. I don't wanna hear it. I have too much on my mind for this shit.
CHRISTIAN: That's all you have to say. I looked death in the eye on the river road. A boy nearly took out my liver with a bayonet. I'm serious. I drop and kiss the ground that he was a romantic, and spared me when I told him I was a man on a mission.

(Mama cracks open a cold beer.)

MAMA: It's cold, why can't you be happy with that?
CHRISTIAN: Because, it isn't what I want? Bring me a Fanta, please.

(Mama smiles and gets him a Fanta.)

MAMA: I'll put on some music.
CHRISTIAN: What's the point, you never dance with me.

(Mama laughs.)

MAMA: Oh shut up, relax. I'll roast some groundnuts. Huh?

(A moment.)

CHRISTIAN: Why not us?
MAMA: What would we do, professor? How would it work? The two of us? Imagine. You'd wander. I'd get impatient. I see how men do. We'd argue, fight and I'd grow resentful. You'd grow jealous. We know this story. It's tiresome.
CHRISTIAN: You know everything, don't you? And if I said, I'd stay, help you run things. Make a legitimate business. A shop. Fix the door. Hang the mirror. Protect you. Make love to you.
MAMA: Do I look like I need protection?
CHRISTIAN: No, but you look like you need someone to make love to you.
MAMA: Do I now?
CHRISTIAN: Yes. How long has it been, Mama, since you allowed a man to touch you? Huh? A man like me, who isn't looking through you for a way home.

(Mama laughs at him.)

MAMA: Enough. God. You're getting pathetic.
CHRISTIAN: Maybe. But damn it against my better judgment . . . I love you.
MAMA *(With contempt)*: Love. What's the point in all this shit? Love is too fragile a sentiment for out here. Think about what happens to the things we "love." It isn't worth it.

"Love." It is a poisonous word. It will change us. It will cost us more than it returns. Don't you think? It'll be an unnecessary burden for people like us. And it'll eventually strangle us!

CHRISTIAN: Do you hear what you're saying?

MAMA: It's the truth. Deal with it!

CHRISTIAN: Hm . . . Why do I bother. If you can't put it on a scale it is nothing, right?! Pardon me.

(Christian, flustered by her response, walks to the door.)

MAMA: Where are you going?!

(Mama watches suddenly panicked.)

Hey! You heard me. Don't be a baby.

(Christian stops before exiting.)

CHRISTIAN: We joke. It's fun. But honestly I'm worn bare. I've been driving this route a long time and I'm getting to the age where I'd like to sleep in the same bed every night. I need familiar company, food that is predictable, conversation that's too easy. If you don't know what I'm talking about, then I'll go. But, please, I'd like to have the truth . . . why not us?

(A moment. Mama says nothing. Christian starts to leave, but her words catch him.)

MAMA *(With surprising vulnerability)*: I'm ruined. *(Louder)* I'm ruined.

(He absorbs her words.)

CHRISTIAN: God, I don't know what those men did to you, but I'm sorry for it. I may be an idiot for saying so, but I think we, and I speak as a man, can do better.

(He goes to comfort her. She pulls away until he's forced to hold her in a tight embrace.)

MAMA: No! Don't touch me! No!

(She struggles to free herself, but eventually succumbs to his heartfelt embrace. She breaks down in tears. He kisses her.)

SOPHIE *(Entering)*: Oh, I'm sorry. *(Smiles to herself)*
MAMA *(Pulling away)*: Why are you standing there looking like a lost elephant.
SOPHIE: Sorry, Mama.

(Sophie slips out.)

MAMA: Don't think this changes anything.
CHRISTIAN: Wait there.
MAMA: Where are you going?

(Christian straightens his suit.)

CHRISTIAN: I swear to you, this is the last time I'll ask.

> A branch lists to and fro,
> An answer to the insurgent wind,
> A circle dance,
> Grace nearly broken,
> But it ends peacefully,
> Stillness welcome.

(Christian holds his hand out to Mama. A moment. Finally, she takes his hand. He pulls her into his arms. They begin to

dance. At first she's a bit stiff and resistant, but slowly she gives in. Possibility. Guitar music: "A Rare Bird" guitar solo. Sophie drags Josephine into the room. They watch the pair dance.)

JOSEPHINE *(Joyfully)*: Go, Mama.
PARROT: Mama! Primus! Mama! Primus!

(Mama and Christian continue their measured dance. The lights slowly fade.)

THE END

In memory of Waple Newton, my grandmother, who introduced me to the art of storytelling. My teacher.

SWAHILI TRANSLATIONS

Atsha makelle	Stop the noise
Banga liwa	Fear death
Funga kinua yaké	Shut her mouth
Karibu	Welcome
Kiwele wele	Dummy
Kuya apa	Come here
Mavi yako	Shit
Modja, mbili, tatu, ine	One, two, three, four
Pumbafu	Stupid
Sante	Cheers
Sasa	Quick
Sawa sawa	Okay okay
Weye	You

SONGS FROM *RUINED*

Original Compositions by
Lynn Nottage, lyrics
Dominic Kanza, music

You Come Here To Forget

Dominic Kanza   Lyrics by Lynn Nottage

have— an oth— er beer____ my friend   douse the fi re of your

fears my friend   get drunk and foo lish   on the mo ment

brush a side the day's hea vy judge ment   yes have an oth er

beer my friend   wipe a way the ang ry   tears my friend

get drunk and foo lish   on the moment

6

Gtr.

you come here to for get   you say drive a way all re

gret   and dance like it's the end ing   the end ing of

the war   and dance like it's the

end ing   the end ing   of the war

and dance like it's the end ing

A Rare Bird

Dominic Kanza   Lyrics by Lynn Nottage

A rare___ bird on a limb sings a___ song___ heard by a few a few pa tient and dis tant listen ers hear it's___sweet sweet song a sound that haunts the

2

forest   a   cry   that tells a

Gtr.

sto ry   har   mon ious   but time for

Gtr.

gott en   to   be ___ seen   is to be

Gtr.

doomed   it must ev   ade   e vade

Gtr.

cap ture   and yet the

Gtr.

bird   still cries out   to be   he ard   and yet the   bird   still cries out   to be

Gtr.

he ard   and yet the   bird   still   cries   out   to   be____

Gtr.

A Warrior

Dominic Kanza   Lyrics by Lynn Nottage

2

and the fo rest de cays

but here   we're pou ring cham pagne

a warr ior knows no   peace   when a hun gry li on's a

wake   but when that li on's a sleep

the warr ior's free to   play   drape your

wear in ess on my shoul der

sweep tra vel dust

from your heart

vi lla ges die

as sol diers grow bol der

we par ty

as the world falls a part

a warr ior knows no peace

4

when a hun gry li on's a wake

Gtr.

but when that li on's a

sleep

Gtr.

the warr ior's free to play

PHOTOGRAPHS

by Tony Gerber

In 2004 and 2005, I traveled to East Africa to conduct interviews with Congolese women fleeing the protracted armed conflict in the Democratic Republic of Congo. The women I interviewed recounted raw and ugly tales of sexual violation and torture at the hands of both Rebel and Government militias. I found my play *Ruined* in their painful narratives, in the gentle cadences and the monumental space between their gasps and sighs. The women felt it was important to go on record, which is why my play is not about victims, but survivors.

Filmmaker Tony Gerber, my husband, took portraits of the women moments after they shared their powerful stories. For more information, please visit his website: www.marketroadfilms.com

—LN

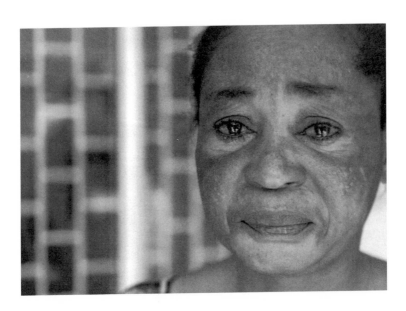

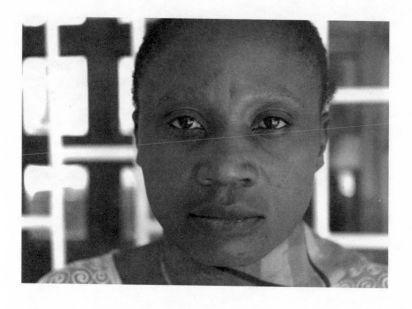

For further information and/or to make contributions, please visit these websites:

Amnesty International
www.amnesty.org

Enough Project
www.enoughproject.org/conflict_areas/eastern_congo

Equality Now
www.equalitynow.org/english/campaigns/african-protocol/african-protocol_en.html

Friends of the Congo
www.friendsofthecongo.org

Global Fund for Women
www.globalfundforwomen.org/cms/issues/overview

Human Rights Watch
www.hrw.org/en/news

International Rescue Committee
www.theirc.org/special-report/congo-forgotten-crisis.html

International Women's Health Coalition
www.iwhc.org

Mapendo International
www.mapendo.org

Peace Women Project: Women's International League for Peace and Freedom
www.peacewomen.org

Raise Hope for Congo
www.raisehopeforcongo.org/solutions

UN Action against Sexual Violence in Conflict
www.stoprapenow.org

VDAY: Sexual Violence in the DRC background
www.vday.org/drcongo/background

Women for Women International
www.womenforwomen.org

Kate Whoriskey, second from left, and Lynn Nottage, far right, with five of the Congolese women who shared their stories.

LYNN NOTTAGE's Pulitzer Prize—winning play *Ruined* has also received an OBIE, the Lucille Lortel Award, New York Drama Critics' Circle Award for Best Play, a Drama Desk and an Outer Critics Circle Award (Manhattan Theatre Club, Goodman Theatre). Other plays include *Intimate Apparel* (New York Drama Critics' Circle Award for Best Play; Roundabout Theatre, CENTERSTAGE, South Coast Repertory); *Fabulation, or The Re-Education of Undine* (OBIE Award; Playwrights Horizons, London's Tricycle Theatre); *Crumbs from the Table of Joy*; *Las Meninas*; *Mud, River, Stone*; *Por'knockers* and *POOF!*

Nottage is the recipient of numerous awards, including the 2007 MacArthur Foundation "Genius Grant," the National Black Theatre Festival's August Wilson Playwriting Award, the 2004 PEN/Laura Pels Award for Drama, the 2005 Guggenheim Grant for Playwriting, as well as fellowships from the Lucille Lortel Foundation, Manhattan Theatre Club, New Dramatists and New York Foundation for the Arts.

Her most recent publications include: *Intimate Apparel and Fabulation, or The Re-Education of Undine: Two Plays* (TCG) and *Crumbs from the Table of Joy and Other Plays* (TCG). She is a member of The Dramatists Guild, an alumna of New Dramatists and a graduate of Brown University and the Yale School of Drama, where she is a visiting lecturer. www.lynnnottage.net